EUGENIA PRICE

traveled widely for twelve years speaking in colleges,
churches and to business and professional groups
throughout the North American continent. Her
transcribed radio series *A Visit With Genie* still has
an extensive audience. She has recorded for Audio-
Bible Society and will soon record for Word Records.
Her first ten books have sold over a million copies
and each has become a best seller. GOD SPEAKS TO
WOMEN TODAY is, in her own words, " . . . a
condensation of all I have learned about God's way
of readjusting a woman's personality so that she can
begin to handle her problems because she has learned
to handle herself."

BOOKS BY EUGENIA PRICE . . .

Discoveries

Never a Dull Moment

Share My Pleasant Stones

What Is God Like?

Beloved World

A Woman's Choice

Find Out for Yourself

God Speaks to Women Today

Woman to Woman

Just As I Am

The Wider Place

Make Love Your Aim

The Unique World of Women

Learning to Live From the Gospels

The Beloved Invader

New Moon Rising

Lighthouse

No Pat Answers

Learning to Live From the Acts

Don Juan McQueen

Maria

St. Simons Memoir

Leave Your Self Alone

Margaret's Story

GOD SPEAKS TO WOMEN TODAY

Eugenia Price

Zondervan Publishing House
Grand Rapids, Michigan

GOD SPEAKS TO WOMEN TODAY

Zondervan Books edition published March 1969

Copyright © 1964 by Zondervan Publishing House

Zondervan Publishing House,
1415 Lake Drive, S.E.,
Grand Rapids, Michigan 49506

Library of Congress Catalog Card Number: 64-9315

ISBN 0-310-31301-5

Printed in the United States of America

84 85 86 87 88 — 50 49 48 47 46 45 44

Contents

PREFACE

For several years I have been asked by women's group leaders (my own mother among them) to write a book suitable for use both as private and group devotional material. Only now have I found what I believe to be the most creative approach to such a book, both in content and form.

Since God never wastes anything, He must have had solid, constructive, practical reasons for giving us, in the Bible, the life stories and experiences of so many different types of women. You are there, and I am there, represented by our particular problems, personality quirks, good points and bad.

If He bothered to see to it that these women are given space in the Bible, it seems to me that it is up to us to learn all we can from them, before running here and there for human help in our daily dilemmas. Before we belabor friends, ministers, and other counselors for quick answers and panaceas for our sorrows and disappointments and troubles, doesn't it make better sense to go to the Word of God first?

Have you ever thought of examining God's actions in the lives of the Bible women for His purpose in your life? Writing this book has been a tremendous eye-opener for me. I have found practical insight not only into my own personality, but also into the personalities of those with whom my life functions. If we study the lives of the Bible women, we have to learn also about their husbands, their children, their relatives and friends. No one lives isolated on an island, remote from other human beings.

It is my sincere hope that your study and use of this book will send you to the actual pages of Scripture for further enlightenment. All pertinent Scripture references are given at the beginning of each chapter, and I have used the *Berkeley Version* when actual Scripture is quoted.

The book is designed so that it will be immediately usable to you in your private devotions and study, as well as in group use. In the case of the longer stories, such as Sarah, Rebekah, Jesus' mother, Mary, etc., you will find the narrative divided into several vignettes, told mainly without comment, in story form. Then, following each vignette, I have written what came to me by way of practical application for our lives as we live them out in the twentieth century. If you are in charge of the devotional portion of a meeting, select the vignette you want, read (or request another woman to read) the story proper, then follow it with your reading of my comments, brightened and strengthened, I hope, by still more light and insight of your own. But if you don't have time to study at all, each section reads no longer than the time usually allotted to devotional leaders.

You will not find all the women of the Bible here. This is not mainly a reference book, although I hope it will be of help to Sunday school and Bible teachers too. But I have made my selections of Bible women according to the relevancy of their problems and joys to ours.

I would hesitate to attempt a book without my mother's prayers, encouragement and always cheerful letters, and I thank God that I have never had to do this. She has backed me up in these good ways through the writing of this one, and she has "tried out" my material with her Sunday school class and in women's meetings. Through the writing of still another book, Joyce Blackburn has not only assisted in research and given her excellent criticism of every line, but has shared both my happy and discouraging hours, and along with my publishers, keeps me believing in my own potential in Jesus Christ.

I am grateful again to Thelma Jennings, who has typed beautifully and carefully perhaps her last manuscript for me, since she leaves soon for the mission field. A heartfelt "thank you" also to my dear friends, Dr. Anna B. Mow and Miss Addison Pelletier for giving me their valid comments on each chapter.

My thanks to all of you who read, and by your letters of encouragement, keep me writing. Most particularly I am grateful to you who asked for this book, and who have prayed for me as I worked.

It is my sincere prayer that He will be able to speak to you personally through the stories of these very human women. As I finished the last chapter, I was convinced that we women are not really a bad lot—even Paul formed deep bonds of friendship with some of the women of the Early Church, and I doubt that the great apostle was prejudiced against us, as so many believe him to have been. I think he truly revered and respected the women who gave him half a chance to respect them! He found the Christ-controlled ladies rather easy to love. This, my friends, can be a big clue for us.

EUGENIA PRICE

Chicago, Illinois
July, 1964

AN INTRODUCTION TO US ALL

Eve—A Woman and a Fatal Conversation

Until Eve had her famed conversation with the tempter that day, the first man and woman moved about to the very rhythm of heaven. At night they slept near each other in quiet, love-filled, dreamless rest. All day long they *lived,* interested and occupied with the gifts around and within them, enjoying each other and enjoying God. When the warm sun cooled and it was evening, they were never weary or bored. They were glad. It was then time for God Himself to visit with them in the perfect home He had given them. They waited for Him, anticipating the first sound of His voice. There was always much to tell Him about their day, and they knew He would always give them His undivided attention. Until Eve had her talk with the tempter, there was no trouble whatever in the Garden of Eden, and no human relationship problems anywhere on the face of the earth. All the trouble began for everyone with the woman called Eve.

God created Adam first, but obviously, this did not place any more responsibility upon the man than upon his wife. God did not expect more of him as a human being than He expected of the woman. They were both created in His own image, and He gave equally to both. To both He offered the perfect atmosphere and environment for a full, creative, joy-filled life on earth. To both He gave the same healthful air to breathe, the same food to eat, the same beauty to enjoy and the same perfect communion with Himself.

To both He gave the same responsibility: obedience to Him as Creator and Father God. They could eat, He told them carefully, from every tree in the garden except one. They did not *need* the fruit of this tree, the tree of knowledge of good and evil, because God Himself knew all there was to know about all things, and trusting Him to guide them was their part in keeping perfect communication between them and the Creator. He asked them to keep away from the fruit of that one tree because He alone knew *how* to distinguish good from evil. With all His heart of love He wanted to guide them in the way that would keep their lives in peace, without tension or struggle. He wanted their home on earth to remain peaceful. In the will of God, all human relationships are harmonious, full of real life and creative. This fact God understood as no one else could ever understand it, because no one else could be God. And so, He did not command them to stay away from the fruit of the tree of the knowledge of good and evil in order to put a damper on their happiness. Rather, He gave them this instruction in order to *protect* for all time, the inner peace and harmony He had given them in the beginning.

The Lord God expected no more from one than from the other. Neither was a divinely created puppet on a wire hooked mechanically to the hand of God. Both were divinely created human beings, attached by love to the heart of God, but recipients of the dangerous and glorious gift of *free choice*. God did all He could do for them, and then He left the final choice of obedience or disobedience to them, to each of them individually. He did not instruct Adam to manage Eve. He did not instruct Eve to manage her husband. To each one, as a separate and morally responsible human being, God said: "Do not touch the fruit of that one tree."

When Eve succumbed to the tempter's clever argument, Adam proved once and for all, that the creature called *woman* holds within her being a particular power to influence.[1] He proved this by succumbing right along with her! He didn't have to do it. He, too, was a creature with free choice; but the fact remains that he did, leaving us to face another irrevocable fact: that while each human being is morally responsible to God for himself alone, women do have a special responsibility to see to it that their lives influence those around them in a way which God can accept.

There is no pat explanation for this fact about the influential natures of women. It does not make us more important than men; but it does indicate that there is a *difference*, such a difference that the tempter went to Eve and

---

[1] See *Woman to Woman*, Eugenia Price, (Zondervan) Chapter 1.

not to her husband. Whether the difference is based on inner weakness or strength is beside the point.

The fact remains that all the trouble in the world began with the one fatal conversation between the woman called Eve and the "wiliest of all the field animals," her tempter. Down through the thousands upon thousands of years of progress and suffering, weeping and joy, through culture upon fallen culture, into the frightening immediacy of this moment, rolls the continuing shock of the fatal outcome of that one conversation!

A woman like yourself, created in God's own image, stopped unsuspectingly one afternoon to listen to an arresting voice and a clever persuasion.

"So, God has told you not to eat from any tree in the garden!"

Eve's answer must have come quickly, naturally, defensive of the Lord God. "Oh, we may eat the fruit of all the garden trees; but about the fruit of the tree in the center of the garden God has said, 'You shall not eat of it or even touch it, lest you die.' "

It is ridiculous to imagine that Eve's tempter was confused. He was not. He knew all along that God had *not* forbidden any other tree. Eve's answer was not, perhaps, so much naive, as still pure. Her moment of sin had not yet come. She simply told the serpent the truth, as one would tell it who had never heard of trickery of any kind. There is also no doubt in my mind but that the tempter knew the true meaning of God's words: ". . . lest you die." Adam and Eve were enjoying the full life, *eternal* life. God had not planned even a physical death for them. But the tempter knew that much more than the potential of physical death lay ahead, should Eve touch and eat the forbidden fruit. The tempter knew that the deepest, most devastating form of death would overtake them. They would be jerking themselves free from the loving control of their Creator. *Spiritual life* would be drained from them. They would be cutting themselves off from the free flowing life of God into their beings. They would be alive only in their bodies and in their minds. Where there had been no barrier between them and God, suddenly a heavy ceiling would lower upon them. They would be forced, by the very lack of communion with Life Himself, to drudgery and sorrow.

The tempter knew this, and so he planned his next approach carefully. "No, you would not die at all! But God knows that when you eat of that tree, your eyes will be opened and you will, like gods, know all good and evil!"

Like gods.

A new, exciting, strident rhythm began to pulse through Eve's being. "Like gods! Adam and I like gods!"

She looked again at the beautiful tree in the center of the garden. The tempter contented himself with silence. It was enough for the moment, that he had persuaded her to look at the tree in this new way. She saw it now, not only as beautiful and belonging to God, but as beautiful and with the potential of belonging to her and to Adam. Until that moment it had never occurred to her to touch even one fruit. Now her whole being hungered for it. Still the serpent kept silent. There was no need to say anything more to this foolish woman. To his cunning mind, it would be only a matter of a few gusts of wind through the high trees until she would bring her husband, too.

Eve ate, and then Adam ate, and it all began right there, for every woman and every man. All their grasping, self-willed human passion began to flow forever through the inner being of everyone who would ever be born into the world.

Adam named his wife, Eve, because that meant *life*. Her life is in us all. Her original capacity for enjoyment is there, but there also is her self-inflicted, capacious greed for replacing the will of God with her own will. Her desire for peace given by her Creator is in us all, and her self-styled bent to chaos; her ability to love and her ability to wound.

Once the fruit was eaten, she stood trembling, ashamed, confused. Eve was no longer one person, at peace with herself and her husband and God. She was two persons, in deadly conflict. A dark stranger had crashed to life within her, and she was afraid. Neither she nor Adam were able to dismiss God from their thoughts. His image was too deeply carved into their beings. They had been created to belong to Him, and they suffered intensely in this new, strange loneliness for Him. It was as though the dark selves newly alive and active within them, battled their once innocent, pure selves. Civil war began to rage within the only two people on earth. It still rages in the earth's people today.

It all began for everyone there. Eve was a real woman, like the women we know and the women we are. We dare not think of this woman called Eve as a remote, unreal creature, shuddering in shame in a mythical paradise. She was the mother of every living person!

What does this really have to do with us? Only everything. God did not heap punishment on the heads of our first parents out of some whim of His own. They had made their choice; He could simply no longer trust them with the original life of joy and happiness and ease. They had broken their connection with God. He did not leave *them,* they jerked themselves free of their own choice. In one sense, Eve "created" the new, troublesome nature within her.

Knowing that we have inherited this nature can surely make us more realistic. We can stop the altogether foolish, egotistical habit of being shocked when we do something that shows us to be less than the splendid creatures we think ourselves to be. We can stop the equally foolish habit of expecting more of those around us than we have a right to expect, knowing that they, too, are the moral and spiritual offspring of this first very human woman. I can't believe it was difficult for Adam and Eve to accept the ugly fact that their first born son, Cain, murdered his gentle brother, Abel. The whole thing was too fresh in their minds. They still remembered their own sin sharply, and they must have been quite realistic about Cain. Hurt, grieved, heartbroken, but realistic, realizing more every day of their lives that man is capable of *anything* evil unless he is at one with the Lord God.

Surely, Eve's fatal conversation with her tempter can make us more realistic, but we dare not stop there. God, in His wide mercy, has seen to it that we need not stop there. He did not just let them wander out of the garden without a word that shadowy afternoon. Not only did He, with His own hands, make garments of skin to cover their nakedness, He spoke clearly of the One who would bring permanent relief from their new darkened confusion. He spoke of the Coming One who would be born of a *woman,* and who would one day crush the head of the serpent who shared that conversation with Eve (Genesis 3:15). As these two frightened sin-diseased, tragic figures walked uncertainly out into a world that would be strange and hard, the Voice they had waited for so expectantly in the cool of the evening called after them a clear note of hope.

The promised Redeemer has come. His name is Jesus Christ. As He provided the perfect life for Adam and Eve in the beginning, God has lovingly provided for us the way back to original oneness with Himself. The dual nature of our mother and father is still in us, but *unification* is possible now. Harmony can return. The way of reconciliation (harmony) has been given to every tortured, twisted, bad-tempered, self-centered, grasping human being on earth. No mother ever needs to be shocked at the conduct of her child, as though *her* offspring should be "above" sin. But neither does she need to despair. The original harmony with the Father can be restored to anyone at anytime, through Jesus Christ. The same quality of *eternal life* which Adam and Eve shared with Him, can be given back to any of us, their children.

Why then, if this is true, is there so little harmony in our homes, our churches, our hearts? Is it because we, as women of the progressive but tormented twentieth century, have considered ourselves remote and removed from the predicament of this first woman named Eve? Do we feel replete and detached in our world of super markets and dacron blouses and space ships? Have we failed to identify with this woman who had the fatal conversation that day in her garden home? Do we, because we live in a somewhat Christian environment, feel ourselves superior to her? Have we ever stopped to pity her? To try to imagine what her moment of shame was really like? One small effort to identify with someone puts us at least briefly in that person's place. And this is where we need to stand perhaps for many long moments—in Eve's place! If we fail to do this, we are being totally unrealistic, because we are her children. We stand guilty beside her; guilty and understandably confused and out of harmony with God. And there we continue to stand until we have accepted (with the same will she used in choosing to disobey, the forgiveness God offers through Jesus Christ, *and* the restored eternal life.

The tempter who persuaded Eve is still hard at work with us. When there are flying tempers and anxiety and gossip and sarcasm and possessiveness, he is winning with us as surely as he won with Eve! But God is at work, too, always moving toward us. What about our response to Him?

No one can sanely argue the fact that Eve knew a kind of pure oneness with God which you and I, because of what she and her husband did, have never known on this earth. But we belittle Christ when we use this as an alibi for character weaknesses and continuing dilemmas. There is available now, to everyone, the potential of the same in-

ner oneness and harmony with God which our first parents
knew. The way back has been offered in the Person of
Jesus, "without whom nothing was made that was made."
The Creator God came Himself to bring us back to Himself.

The door to the garden is no longer closed.

1. SARAH

God's Woman in Spite of Herself

Sarai had never looked more beautiful to her husband, Abram, than the day he surprised her as she broke the long stems of an armful of lilies to fit her favorite chased brass vase in the dining room of her home in Ur.

"I have something important to tell you, Sarai."

Ordinarily she would have kept right on arranging her flowers as she talked to Abram. This time the solemn note in his voice drew her full attention. They faced each other for a long moment, Sarai puzzled by the new certainty on his strong, bearded face, for once not prodding him to speak.

"We're going to leave Ur, Sarai. God spoke to me, and told me to go."

She leaned against the heavy, ornate table where her flowers lay, half in and half out of the vase. She was sixty-five and Abram ten years older. They had lived all their lives in this bustling, metropolitan city of Ur in Mesopotamia. Their friends were all here. Abram's business was here. His father, Terah, was one of the leading idol makers. His brothers and their families were here. Why would they want to leave?

"God spoke to me, Sarai. He told me to go." Without waiting for her reaction, as he usually did, Abram went on talking quietly, as though they had been in long conversation. "As clearly as a man can hear, I heard the voice of the true God say to me: 'As for you, leave your land, your relatives and your father's household for a land which I will show you, and I will make you into a great nation.' "

. A geat nation? How could Abram's God do this when Sarai, at sixty-five, had never given her husband a child!

"I do not understand it, Sarai, but He has spoken, and I cannot refuse to obey Him."

This time, perhaps the first time in their married lives, Abram was not asking her opinion. He was stating a fact. They were going. There seemed to be no choice. He was not brusque, merely strong with the strange, new certainty. With no argument, Sarai began making plans to break up her comfortable home. She saw that their portable belongings were packed, and piece by beloved piece, she watched her magnificent, hand-carved furniture being sold or given away. She sorted her linens, gave the perplexed servants endless orders, sent messages to friends explaining almost nothing, and watched the familiar possessions disappear through the courtyard of her home.

The sorrow at leaving Ur was added to early in their strange journey, when Abram's brother, and then his father, Terah, died. But on went Abram and Sarai, their caravan of pack and riding beasts, servants, and the remaining members of their family, including Abram's nephew, Lot, without the solace of being able to say, "In three months or three years we will reach our destination and this will end." Only the Lord God knew when it would end. They could only keep moving slowly through the dry, hot days, along the level banks of the Euphrates River, around the Fertile Crescent, to the trail leading south along the Mediterranean Sea, one hard day following another, with everything strange and no end in sight. A 65-year-old woman and her 75-year-old husband, forced to change the entire pattern of their lives from comfortable city-dwellers to semi-nomads of the desert. The most Sarai could hope for now was a large black goats-hair tent!

*　　　*　　　*

Was the idea of Sarai in a goats-hair tent as strange and cumbersome to her as it would be to us today? I believe it was. Their home city of Ur was highly civilized; its wealthy citizens lived in luxury. Idol makers were prosperous men, and Abram's father was one of the leading idol makers of Ur. Sarai had friends to admire her beauty, and expensive clothes to accentuate it. She was the mistress of a two-storied, balconied house, with a courtyard full of flowers and palms. She had servants to dress her, prepare her food and clean her home. There were thick, silky, oriental rugs on her polished stone floors. It is quite likely that Sarai lived what we would call a "socialite" existence.

Could we leave luxury like that for a life of packing and unpacking, as camels and donkeys dragged us and our few remaining belongings here and there across an almost trackless, arid, semi-desert land? *Would* we do it? Would you inform your husband that he had lost his mind even to ask you? No one could blame Sarai if she had thought this. After all, the Biblical account clearly indicates that Sarai and her husband normally talked things over together. He considered her his equal, and yet point blank, he was asking her to leave their comfortable city home and become a wanderer. There is nothing to indicate that Sarai was a timid woman, either. Her later actions prove her to have been not only highly intelligent, but highly opinionated. Knowing this, do you think Abram must have trembled a bit to ask her? How would your husband react in the same situation? Does he have reason to trust your elasticity in the face of his quickly changed plans?

We are not given any of these details, but if Sarai did lose her temper at first, apparently she regained it and went diligently about the heartbreaking and confusing business of breaking up her beautiful home, so that her husband was *not* forced by her self-centeredness to disobey God. Abram apparently could trust Sarai's emotional equilibrium under fire!

They had undoubtedly heard the ancient story of Adam and Eve; they knew they were descendants of Noah, but Abram's father was an idol maker, and the deity of the people of Ur was the moon-goddess, Nana. Where did Abram and Sarai come by the kind of faith that would permit blind obedience of an unexplained command from the true God? Don't forget, they had no Scriptures; they had heard no sermons; they had read no books about the potential of the life of God within the human personality. They could not have known exactly what was happening in the divine Plan, and yet their behavior proves that almost without their realizing it, He had planted the seed of His own life within them! Abram, a steady man, uprooted his entire household. Sarai, an opinionated woman, went submissively. *We* know in retrospect of His plan to bring the Coming One, promised to Adam and Eve. They could not have known, and yet God was able to hold their hearts and their confusions under His control.

Perhaps even more amazing than her willingness to break up her home, was Sarai's willingness to move on, not knowing where they would stop. A woman's home can hold her very identity in the shape and texture of its rooms. Even in the twentieth century, when the earth's people move at random by plane, train, station wagon and cross-country van, women's hearts are wrenched at the sudden news that their husband's military or business transfer necessitates a move. At least today's woman knows where she is going. There will be a house of some kind at the end of the journey; there *will* be a destination. Only God knew where Abram and Sarai were going. He had put them in the glorious predicament of having to trust Him!

Can we make use of the same elasticity of spirit and mind that Sarai used? If not, we are underestimating God Himself. She could do it, all those centuries ago, in the semi-twilight of His revelation of Himself. Knowing Him in Jesus Christ as we do, are we adventurous enough to Him to be *God's women*, in spite of ourselves?

Running Ahead of God

Sarai's capable and beautiful new Egyptian maid, Hagar, moved easily about the big black tent, spreading a fresh bed for her mistress. Neither woman had spoken for several minutes. Sarai's anxious mind was turning this way and that, considering the strange, troubling events of their recent detour into the fertile land of Egypt when a famine struck Canaan. It had turned out all right, she supposed, in spite of the fact that Abram had taken a dreadful chance of losing her forever when he told the Pharaoh she was his sister. Of course, she was his half-sister, but how could Abram—gentle, considerate Abram—actually allow her to be taken because of her still high beauty, into the Pharaoh's palace in order to save his own neck?

"Anyone knows you're a good-looking woman," he had said, rising up beside her on his tall camel as they entered Egypt. "When these Egyptians catch sight of you, I'll be in trouble. They're sure to say, 'So, this beautiful, fair-skinned woman is his wife! We'll kill the man and keep the woman alive.' So, I want you to say you're my sister. That way, I'll even be favored because of your beauty."

At her age, it was good to hear her husband call her beautiful; gratitude swelled in her heart for this, and for his constant devotion to her through the years, even though she had never given him a child. She couldn't refuse his request, and he had guessed correctly: The Pharaoh, himself, took Sarai into his palace (loading Abram with expensive gifts), but her days there were days of mounting fear and anxiety, in spite of the luxurious life among his other wives and concubines. Every day she was sure Pharaoh would call *her,* and her heart longed for the safety and shelter of her goats-hair tent—and her own husband beside her. One thought still tormented her: had this been Abram's way of being rid of her so that another woman could give him a child?

She jerked herself back to the safety and goodness of today. Hagar, the young slave girl given her by the Pharaoh when they left Egypt at last, stood waiting for Sarai's next order. They had left the pagan land, both alive, because the Pharaoh felt their presence brought the sickness that struck most of Egypt. She was at home now in her own tent, back in the land of Canaan. God had protected them once more. She must stop worrying and just be glad.

Sarai motioned toward the smoke-blackened, goat-skin water bottles, and Hagar began to fill the pitchers from them. Still neither woman spoke. Hagar was an excellent servant who respected her mistress' moods. Excellent, industrious, beautiful—young. Young. Sarai was old, too old now ever to give Abram an heir, no matter how often her husband had tried to reassure her of God's promise to make them both a great nation. *Dear, kind Abram,* she thought, *and I doubted his intentions toward me in Egypt. Right or wrong, he seems loyal to me, his childless, barren, useless wife!* Her old, wearing pain was still there, sharper than ever before. In her marriage contract, she had promised him an heir. Customarily, any other woman would have provided the child, even if through one of her trusted slave girls.

Hagar smoothed Sarai's bed and gestured gracefully toward it. The older woman stared at her, her mind tossing its sudden scheme back and forth crazily: a scheme still safe in her thoughts only. But, it *was* there. This young girl was a comparatively new slave. To choose her would be less embarrassing than choosing one brought with her from Ur. Lot's wife was gone now, too; she despised that arrogant young woman. Abram unselfishly had allowed Lot to choose the best of the land, and Lot, opportunist that he was, chose the well-watered Jordan district and left, taking his family with him. But, wait—the very day Lot's caravan disappeared from sight, Abram had heard from the Lord again: "Now, Abram, raise your eyes and look from where you stand northward, southward, eastward and westward, for all the land you are viewing I will give you and your offspring forever."

Offspring? Abram's offspring? His descendants were to

be as countless as the dust of the earth, he told her—the Lord's exact words to him that day. Too fantastic! Sarai stood up abruptly.

"Hagar?"

"Yes, Mistress."

"Hagar, perhaps it is God's will that I swallow my pride and allow my husband to have this child by another woman—you!" The dread scheme was no longer safe inside Sarai's mind. Hagar stared at her mistress. "I trust you Hagar. You are my faithful servant. I now elevate you to being the master's concubine. See that you give him an heir!"

Even Abram seemed not to detect the fresh agony in his wife, when he agreed to go through with her plan. Hagar went in to Abram, and from that day nothing was ever the same again between her and Sarai. At first, there was only Sarai's keen gaze following her at her work. Of course, no one was sure yet that she would bear him a child either, and the old woman reproached herself at night in her bed for hoping that Hagar too might fail. One day the reproaches stopped; there was no longer a reason for them. Hagar was going to give Abram a child, and Sarai's jealousy and shame grew as the news spread over the large encampment. Almost overnight Hagar had begun to be what Sarai had never known her to be—arrogant, haughty, cruel. A new, flippant, disdainful handmaiden spread her mistress' bed now, sometimes bothering to answer when Sarai called, more often not.

Sarai's fury flared at Abram: "May the injury I suffer come home to you! I entrusted my maid to your bosom and as soon as she found herself with child she looked down on me. Let the Lord do justice between you and me!"

In the face of her unreasonableness, Abram still considered her his equal. "Look, your maid is in your power; handle her as you please, Sarai."

Her husband's words fanned her fury, and she began to mistreat Hagar so mercilessly, that the girl's high spirit was quickly broken. In a panic of fear for herself and her unborn child, Hagar took a small amount of food, strapped a black skin water bottle on her back, and ran away into the desert to escape her once kind mistress, turned tormentor.

*   *   *

In the strictest sense of the word, no woman today

would find herself in exactly the same position as Sarai here. Still, behind her actions lie the principles of jealousy and vengeance—of blame-shifting, of refusing to accept responsibility for decisions which we ourselves make; for *running ahead of God.*

It is true that in Sarai's marriage contract, she undoubtedly had promised an heir to her husband. The custom dictated that if the wife could not bear a child, then she must arrange for the service of someone who could. One word in Sarai's defense here, however: the average woman of her time would not have minded as she did. Most marriages then were marriages of convenience; Sarai and Abram obviously loved each other. Sarai was understandably jealous of Hagar, not only for her youth, but because she succeeded where Sarai had failed so miserably for so many long years.

However, when Hagar turned almost overnight from a loyal, comforting servant into a flippant, haughty woman—in other words, when a part of Sarai's own plan backfired, she took it out on Abram! There is no indication whatever, that Abram in any way changed in his devotion to Sarai. He had merely gone through with her plan. If anything, he had allowed his wife to influence him to act against the promise of God. If a woman exerts Sarai's kind of influence over her husband, the least she can do is assume some responsibility for the decisions she maneuvers. What Sarai did, today's woman might easily do. As soon as she began to feel the sting of her decision, she blamed Abram. "May the injury I suffered come home to you! I entrusted my maid to your bosom and now look how she's treating me!" Somehow it was now all Abram's fault.

While we can certainly sympathize, even empathize with poor Sarai in her deep sense of failure as a wife, the underlying principle remains the same: She made a decision, and when it boomeranged on *her,* she shifted the blame to Abram, refusing to accept responsibility for her own original idea.

We must, of course, always keep in mind the fact that both Abram and Sarai lived thousands of years before God revealed Himself in Jesus Christ. Abram obviously tried to convince Sarai that God would keep His promise to give them an heir. I'm convinced Abram really believed this with most of his heart. I'm sure Sarai wanted to believe it, but to her practical mind, the *facts* were all against it: she was just too old. And so, she figured, before Abram was too old also, they had better do the practical thing and help God along. What she decided to do, in view of the custom of their day, was common practice; but running ahead of God, as they both did, brought the inevitable consequence —trouble all around for everyone. Sarai, striving to do right by her husband, lost all control and performed at her worst before him. Abram, a sensitive man before God, must have grieved that he had agreed in the first place. And Hagar, a non-believer from a pagan country, became the hapless victim of the entire plot.

Once more, we must remember God had not revealed Himself yet in Jesus Christ. A woman today who runs ahead of God, as Sarai did, has even less excuse than she had. Without a doubt, her biggest wrong was in her refusal to wait for God to work out His own plan. This running ahead of Him invariably ends in more stress on the human personality than it can bear. When we "play God" we ultimately put ourselves in the untenable position of facing our lack of self-control. Sarai lost control of herself in the face of what she herself had decided to do. But this loss of self-control is usually the inevitable result of running ahead of God.

Jesus Christ has now come. We have no alibi whatever for not knowing Him to be a God of His Word. It should come as a surprise to no one that women today lose control of their personalities as Sarai did, when they run ahead of God. Only He is God, and only His timing is always right.

God Remembered One Slave Girl

Alone in a strange land, with even her mistress turned tormentor, the child Hagar carried became her very life. Each day she awoke to a fresh agony and impending brutality, and at last the day came when Hagar, fearing for the life of her child, ran away. Somehow she must find her way back across the desert to her homeland. With all her young heart she wanted to live for the child's sake, but within a few hours after she began her flight across the hot, hard ground, she fell, exhausted, beside the first spring of water.

Her unborn child stirred and stretched within her, but she could only lie there, holding the helpless mound of life, fighting her panic and despair. She was thirsty, the spring was there, but there was no energy to drink. A little rest, maybe, and then she could reach for the water. She needed a drink of water; she needed bread. The child would need her to eat. But she could only lie there and refuse to think where she might find food in this wasteland, tomorrow and tomorrow and then tomorrow. Now it was *now*. She must only lie still and rest. Rest in the silence of the darkening sand and sky, with Sarai's tormenting voice too far away to wound her again. Rest here, dazed and alone, except for her child.

"Hagar."

The girl sat up. She was not alone!

"Hagar."

The Voice she heard was like none she had ever known before. A voice to listen for, not to flee from. She dragged herself to her knees, and there she saw Him lighting the rapid desert shadows with His own light: a cool light, with no pain in it, as the desert sun had pained her all day.

She sighed like a small child who had finished the long run home. Was she awake? Was the strength returning to her aching body real? Strength in which she could walk? Strength in which she could think and feel again? Was He real? There He stood beside her, unlike any man she had ever seen in her life, but she felt no strangeness with Him!

"Hagar, Sarai's maid, where have you come from and where are you going?"

How did He know she was Sarai's maid? How did He know her name? Quickly, both questions seemed wrong. She sighed again like the small child who had finished the long run home, knowing more surely than she had ever known anything that He possessed full knowledge of her. Knowing she would *have* to tell Him the truth, she grew still more rested by the knowing.

"I am running away from my mistress, Sarai."

"Go back to your mistress and humble yourself under her authority," He said quietly, understanding about Sarai and about her. "I will greatly increase your descendants beyond all counting, they will be so numerous. You are with child and you will give birth to a son, whom you will name Ishmael, which means *God has heard*."

Hagar was standing up now facing Him.

"Thou seeing God!" she said, forgetting herself entirely. "Thou seeing God!"

He was soon gone, but Hagar thought of only one thing as she trudged unafraid through the dark night, back to

Sarai's tent: "Have I really seen God and remained alive after seeing Him?"

She had, and she named the spring by which He found her Beer-Lahai-Roi, which means, "Well of the living One who sees me."

*   *   *

Would God become a Man so that one frightened, proud, confused Egyptian girl could be sure that He watched over her, too? Would the Eternal take on visible form for a pagan girl whose arrogant behavior had driven His chosen Sarai to such cruelty? Yes, He would. He did.

The story of Hagar is to me one of the most vivid declarations of the intentions of God toward the entire human race. He appeared to Hagar in the desert as surely as He appeared to the eleven in the locked upper room after His Resurrection; as surely as He appeared to the two on the road to Emmaus; to Saul on his way to Damascus; to the five hundred; to His brother, James.

Hagar's need brought Him to her, as surely as our need brings Him to us now. *Nothing else is required*. Great faith is not required, only need. Hagar was a slave-girl from a godless nation. She had found no real refuge on earth and her need brought her face to face with the "Living One who saw her."

We dare not underestimate the yearning of God. He had chosen Sarai and Abram to work out His plan of redemption through Jesus Christ, but this does not mean He loved them any more than He loved Hagar. This does not mean He yearned more over them than over the desperate Egyptian bondslave.

In her need only, He came to her. She saw Him, she believed Him and she was His consciously. Is this farfetched? Dare we call it unorthodox to say that little Hagar met Christ in the shadows of the desert that evening? It was apparently not His plan for her to give Abram his heir, but did God hold this over Hagar's head? Does the God you follow hold it over the ignorant heads of those who do not know Him when you and I run ahead as Abram and Sarai obviously did? He does not. With all my heart, I believe He *did* understand about Sarai and about Hagar. He understands about us all, and yet on He goes with His gloriously relentless plan of redemption, in spite of our ignorant mixed motives and impatience.

On rolled the redemptive plan of God through the very human lives of Sarai and Abram to its completion in Jesus Christ, but Christ—the Word of God—*has been* from the beginning. He *is* the beginning, and He came to Hagar that day in the wilderness, because she was in total need. He bothered to make Himself visible to this simple girl, and she *saw* Him. And because she saw Him, she received the courage to trudge back into the storm of Sarai's ugly rage.

As she walked back over the long miles, her heart asked the question, "Have I really seen God and remained alive after seeing Him?" So great was the darkness in the human mind and heart before Jesus Christ came, this girl could only have questioned as she did. But we know now, that we only *come alive* after we see Him!

We have no way of knowing how much help Sarai and Abram, the believers in the true God, gave this girl after her experience with Him in the desert, but we know she obeyed Him. Her son was named Ishmael, as He instructed her that day.

God's heart has not changed during the centuries between women today and that young woman alone by the spring of water. Think on that heart of His. Think on it and then depend upon it with all your heart.

Child of Laughter

"Shall a child be born to a hundred-year-old man, or can Sarah bear at ninety?" Abraham repeated his question to the Lord God and laughed. His name had been changed to Abraham, "father of a multitude," by the Lord Himself, and Sarai's name had been changed to Sarah. Still they were not convinced that at their advanced ages they could become parents. By now, with his son Ishmael thirteen years old, Abraham could have believed the boy to be God's promised heir. But why did the Lord God come again and again to renew His promise if the heir had already come?

God's answer was firm. "Sarah, your wife is about to bear you a son and you will name him Isaac. With him, too, I will establish My covenant as an everlasting covenant for his children after him."

Early one afternoon, Abraham sat in his tent door, seeking the only shade in this hottest part of the day, pondering what God had said to him. The old man heard no one approach, but when he raised his head from his hands, there, standing a little way from the tent door, were three magnificent-looking men. After the visitors had been fed a good meal, Sarah and Hagar (now somewhat reconciled with the years) stood eavesdropping inside the big black tent, out of sight, as was the custom with women. Hagar particularly kept trying to see one of the visitors without being seen herself. His Voice she knew was the Voice of the One who came to her that day in the wilderness before her son, Ishmael, was born! Her heart pounded with excitement as He spoke again: "Abraham, where is your wife, Sarah?"

"There in the tent, honored visitor."

"Without fail, Abraham, I shall come back to you at the reviving season and Sarah, your wife, will have a son."

When old Sarah began to laugh aloud, Hagar jumped back out of sight. Surely they would hear her aging mistress' shrill, cackling laughter!

"Such a thing for me, worn out as I am? And my husband a hundred years old?" Sarah laughed and laughed, out of control.

The Visitor, whose Voice Hagar remembered, was silent during Sarah's outburst, then He said: "Abraham, why did Sarah laugh just then, saying, 'How could I possibly bear a child, old as I am?' Is anything beyond the Lord's reach? At the appointed time I will return to you, in the spring, and Sarah will have a son."

On the miracle night when Sarah's son was born, there was more laughter in Abraham's encampment. This time, it was believing laughter, because she and Abraham at last had their own child.

"We will call him Isaac, Sarah," her husband said, "because Isaac means—laughter."

When the boy, Isaac, was five, on the day of his weaning feast, his teen-aged half brother, Ishmael, did the wrong thing. It had never been hard for Ishmael to do the wrong thing in Sarah's eyes. On this day of days for the old woman, Ishmael laughed and teased young Isaac, and Sarah's anger rocketed again. Once more, she took it out on Abraham: "No son of a heathen slave woman is going to make fun of my son! *Isaac* is God's promised heir. I want that slave and her big, ugly, rough child out of here! Send both of them away—now."

Early the next morning, Hagar and her son, Ishmael, carrying food and water tearfully given to them by

Abraham, began their long walk away, across the Beer-sheba desert. On the third day, Ishmael dropped first. The water was gone. So was their food. Hagar's love for the boy, more than her physical strength, enabled her to drag him to the scant shade of a dry, dusty desert shrub to die. Neither had spoken for a long time. They were just together, facing the forsaken end of their strange lives. Hagar turned suddenly, stumbled away the distance an arrow flies, before she, too, fell exhausted.

"I cannot watch him die!" Maybe Ishmael heard her, maybe not. She hoped not, as she lay weeping into the rocky ground.

And then over the sound of her weeping there once more came the Voice.

"Hagar." If she raised her head to look, would He be there again? Gentle, insistent, He went on: "Have no fear, God has heard the lad's voice over there where he is."

Hagar raised her head. This time she saw no one, but His Voice was all around her. Above her, cooling the sun; beneath her, softening the dry earth; within her, helping her to believe.

"Have no fear, Hagar. God has heard the lad's voice there where he is. Rise up! Go lift the boy up and hold him by the hand, for I will make him into a great nation."

Ishmael grew up and lived in the Paran desert, becoming an expert hunter, and his mother got him a wife from her native land of Egypt. Today, Arabians who follow the Moslem faith believe they are descended from Ishmael, the cast-out son of Abraham, who, as a teen-ager, called on the Lord God for help as he and his frightened mother, Hagar, lay dying in the desert of Beersheba.

*   *   *

Much had been written about the faith and lack of faith of Sarah and Abraham, where their own child, Isaac, was concerned. Here, it seems to me, we should dwell on one major characteristic of God Himself: in spite of their laughter at His promise, He kept His promise. In spite of the fact that Ishmael had been born out of a deliberate act which sprang from human manipulation, God continued His watch over the boy and his slave mother, Hagar. God's plan to redeem His world had been set in motion in the courts of heaven! It might have moved faster, had there been more human insight and faith in operation; but the plan moved anyway. God's omnipotence shines here brighter than the desert sun. It is more to be considered than their faith or lack of it.

Sarah had not yet, even at ninety, learned how to make use of God's power to control her uneven disposition. Still God gave her the promised heir. As with us today, Sarah must have been aware of the contradictory sides of her personality. She and Hagar apparently got along rather well (at least there are no recorded crises between them), until Ismael laughed at little Isaac on his weaning day. When this happened, Sarah's possessiveness took over and out went both Ishmael and his mother. They could not merely move to another part of town; there was only wilderness around the camp of Abraham in Canaan. When she forced Abraham to send them away, it amounted to sending them to their deaths. But once more, God intervened with Hagar, sensing her desperation, supplying her need.

All of these people were contradictory personalities—as we are. Where they showed great lacks, they also showed true values. Abraham must have taught his son Ishmael well. The boy apparently believed in the Lord God. It was Ishmael's prayer God answered in the desert that day. And yet, we are told that the lad was "a wild ass of a man." More human contradictions: virtues and sins. There is no way possible in which we can extract the most from this story unless we learn to accept Abraham and Sarah, Hagar and Ishmael, as mere human beings, with faults *and* virtues not unlike our own.

But we dare not stop here. God's plan *was* in motion. God Himself was in motion, not only toward them, but toward the whole human race. The tragedy of Eden was going to be redeemed! That He made use of sometimes faith-filled and sometimes faithless, sometimes strong and sometimes weak, human beings is our key to seeing Him still in motion toward us in our dilemmas today.

Sarah and Abraham were not the leading characters in this drama—God was. Their story is more than factual human history, it is the beginning of the story of God in loving action toward His whole beloved world, good and bad, sinful and righteous, controlled and uncontrolled, sick and well, full of tears and laughter.

And He is still in motion toward us today—in the same relentless way of love.

God Got Through to Them Both

In her nineties, and after the piled up years of dreaming and longing for a child of her own, Sarah must have had to exert constant control not to spoil this cherished lad, Isaac. Over and over Sarah and Abraham agreed they had never seen such a beautiful man child. Isaac grew to be a handsome boy, who laughed easily and obeyed his parents as though it made him happy to do it.

Then one day, when Isaac was in his teens, God spoke to Abraham again; and this time, without telling Sarah any details, the old man set off one morning with Isaac and two men servants, to make a sacrifice to God on Mount Moriah, a three days' journey away.

Sarah walked to the edge of their encampment with them. Why was Abraham so secretive? Why did his usually calm, weather-beaten old face show first courage and then terror, as he prepared to leave? Why hadn't he shared God's message with her? Surely her husband was acting on a word from the Lord; she had come to expect this now and to revere Abraham's friendship with God. But what was the word? Why did she feel the clutching anxiety that kept her from smiling as she waved good-by? Why could he not give her some word of comfort as he always did? Abraham looked at her deeply for a moment before he walked away, but he left her only pain in his eyes to remember. What kind of pain was it? Was he still carrying the sting of losing Ishmael? She had felt this old wound healed, but did Abraham still long over his strange, wild-mannered, willful first-born son? She had sent Hagar away with Abraham's permission; what caused his pain this morning? Why was he acting strangely again?

The sun came and went twice, but Sarah knew only the darkness of the stretching foreboding that hung around her like her big black tent. Was it her age that made her so terrified of this mysterious journey? As the hours dragged by, her anxiety turned to dread, and on the third day, when she knew they would have arrived at Mount Moriah, the dread turned to near grief.

She spoke to no one; she ate nothing. Over and over she

tried to reason with herself: nothing but danger to her beloved son, Isaac, could strangle her with this kind of terror and grief, and Isaac was safe with his father! They were only on a short journey, to make a sacrifice to the Lord God. Only a three days' journey away . . . She was getting old and overly imaginative. It is always more difficult for an old, old woman to control her feelings, she reasoned, but her reasoning did not quiet her.

She lay exhausted on her pallet of rugs, two servants standing helplessly by, scarcely daring to speak to her. Suddenly the heavy, hot afternoon lull was shattered by Sarah's scream! She sat bolt upright and pressed her thin old hands over her eyes as though to shut out a sight she could not bear to see.

Three days' journey away, in a thicket on the side of Mount Morah, the sunlit slope sliding away to the quiet valley below, Sarah's husband Abraham raised his long knife above their beautiful son, Isaac, whom he had bound to the wood on the altar they had just built together. Sarah's son said nothing, but God was in his look as his father stood above him, his knife ready to make its stroke.

"Abraham! Abraham!" The familiar Voice rolled commandingly across the silence around them. "Do not lay hands on the lad. Do nothing to him! For now I know that you revere God. You have not held back from Me your only son, your beloved one."

Sarah's thin body sagged; the servants supported her bent shoulders as they laid her gently down again on the thick, brightly colored rugs and bathed her face. At first they thought she was dead, but then they saw her smile quietly, and realized she had only fallen asleep, as a child goes to sleep.

When Abraham and Isaac came home, she was ready for them and for their strange and beautiful story of how the Lord God had provided His own sacrifice—a ram caught in a thicket on Mount Moriah—at the very moment Abraham raised his knife.

Abraham must have wondered at her calm reception of their story, but her mother heart, tending to over-adore this child of her old age, had been prepared by the same Lord who had provided His own sacrifice.

Both men returned closer to God than ever before, to find Sarah closer, too, ready now and prepared for the remaining years of her long, long life, to live as the Lord

God longed for her to live, adequate in His strength, or the sorrow and the joy of her days on earth.

*   *   *

In the Biblical account there is no mention of another major crisis in the life of Abraham's wife, Sarah. Apparently God *had* prepared her for the remaining years of her long, long life. I believe He would have prepared her sooner, had Sarah been less opinionated, less obstinate. Does this sound familiar? Isn't it still true that many of the bumps and jolts in a woman's life are direct consequences of her own self-centered decisions, her own actions and reactions? All understandable, perhaps—as with Sarah. But *our* responsibilities, just the same. "I know the thoughts I think toward you," God said. "They are thoughts of peace and not of evil, to give you an expected end." The "end" God expects for us is one of *inward peace.* Our external circumstances will not always be peace-inducing, but we can live adequate to them, if we have begun to cooperate with God (as Sarah obviously at last began to do) in the midst of them.

It is too imaginative to suppose that the near-death of her beloved Isaac brought her to the place of being totally God's woman—in spite of herself? True, the Bible does not tell us that Sarah experienced the kind of extra-sensory perception we described, at the moment her husband raised his knife to kill Isaac, but is this really far-fetched? Don't most mothers sense when danger strikes their children? Especially when the relationship between a mother and her child is as close as that between Sarah and Isaac? The remainder of Isaac's story indicates that he was an extremely amiable person, obedient and devoted to God and to his parents. Sarah must have adored him, too much, perhaps. It is certainly understandable if she did. The child was a long time coming, and she was an old, old woman. In old age, introspection is natural; the people whom we love become more essential to our happiness. Her life must have centered around Isaac, this miracle child of her old age. But God got through to her, just as surely as He got through to Abraham that day on Mount Moriah, with His true intentions in their lives.

The Lord God wanted Sarah and Abraham to worship *Him,* not Isaac. The remainder of their long lives suggests that they did. We think rightly of Abraham as the first man of great faith, of Sarah, as the first woman of great faith. They were. And yet God had to bring them both to a still deeper place of obedience.

They both came to that place at last, and their remaining years were peaceful. Ours can be, too, if, like Sarah, we move toward full cooperation with the Lord God.

2. LOT'S WIFE

A Woman Chained to Her Past

Lot and his wife and family had been part of the great adventure along with Abraham and Sarah from the time they left Ur of the Chaldees. They went too, not knowing where they were going, and there is no record that either Lot or his wife rebelled at the idea. They left behind them as much as Sarah and Abraham left, but their later actions indicate that the younger couple felt it was expedient that they go. His uncle, Abraham, would be head of the household at the death of Lot's aging grandfather, Terah, and his agile mind told him he had better stay close to his aunt and uncle for his own good.

When Terah died, Abraham and Lot moved out together, at the head of their long caravan of slaves and pack animals and herds, and as they traveled, they prospered more and more until one day trouble broke out among their herdsmen. Lot's men began to harass Abraham's shepherds over the shortage of pastureland. They had prospered so greatly, that there was simply not room enough for both herds. Up to this point, although they owned their possessions separately, Lot and his uncle had kept harmony between them, but now the hungry cattle and sheep jostled for room in the fertile valley where they were encamped, and Abraham had to take action.

"Please, nephew," Abraham said, "let there be no disputing between you and me or between my herdsmen and yours, for we are kinsmen." Abraham loved Lot as his own son, but in his maturing faith in God, the old man saw that they must separate. "Do not despair over this trouble, Lot; is not the whole country open to you? I wish, boy, that you might separate yourself from me now. If you turn to the left, then I will turn to the right. Or if you turn to the right, then I will turn to the left."

The young man was so surprised at his uncle's generosity, he could not answer him at first. "There must

35

be no more trouble between us, Lot. Make your decision now."

"Do you mean, Uncle, that you are giving me my choice of which land to take?"

"I would not have spoken as I did otherwise, Lot. Go take a good look, and let me know which land you decide you want."

Like Abraham, Lot also talked things over with his wife, and together they took a good look and saw how well-watered the whole Jordan district was as far away as Zoar. It seemed to them to be as lush and fruitful as the Garden of Eden must have been. So, without a moment's hesitation, Lot chose the whole Jordan basin for himself and his family.

Excitedly and quickly, Lot and his wife supervised the packing of their belongings, and lined up their camels and donkeys and herds, as Sarah and Abraham watched with heavy hearts. Lot managed a courteous farewell, but plainly he was as eager as his wife to be off to their new, even more prosperous life. As she rode past the old couple standing in the hot morning sun outside their tent, Lot's young wife didn't even bother to look back. Her heart and her interest were up ahead now, where things would have to be better and better for her and her family.

"Lot pitched his tent toward Sodom" at first, but as the months went by his herds increased rapidly because of the ample water and pasture grass, and soon they built a magnificent stone mansion in the city of Sodom itself, where wealth and self-centered, luxurious living absorbed Lot's wife utterly.

If she had ever believed in the Lord God of Abraham, she forgot Him now. Her daughters married pagan men of Sodom, and for the first time in her life, she was surrounded and glutted with all the luxury she had always dreamed of having. Lot's wife loved her life in the evil city. There is no indication that she had the slightest misgiving about it. Money and possessions and social prestige had become her gods and she loved her gods and worshiped them with all her heart.

And then the Angel of the Lord visited Abraham and told him Sodom was going to be destroyed because of its decadence. Fervently, the old man prayed that God would spare Lot and his family. God answered Abraham's prayer, but even as an angel led the members of Lot's household out of the city before the destruction came, the woman Lot had married hated every step she took away from the place where she had been so happy. She was leaving because her husband had commanded her to go, but she could not look ahead this time. Her camel moved forward, but Lot's wife kept her eyes turned back toward Sodom. The big animal carried her away, but she was powerless not to look back at her city as long as she could. Lot watched the crowded road ahead away from the city, but his wife, lunging along gracelessly behind him, kept looking back, and she died that way and became a pillar of salt as the destruction fell on the city she loved.

*   *   *

Much has been written about the selfish nature of Lot's wife. She has remained famous through the centuries as a woman who ate and drank and reveled in the luxuries of the world in rebellion against the Lord God. Literally, she lived for the things of the world: money, rich gowns, lavish furniture, a big home, too much food and wine. A woman who refused all attempts to save her from destruction, she clung willfully and stubbornly to her self-centered interests. This is all true of Lot's wife, but I believe there is still more for us here than a sharp warning to turn from satiation by luxury to salvation by love. This is here, without a doubt, but there is more. Something more subtle, something easier to miss in a superficial reading of this short biography of a selfish woman.

Merely to look back, to remember, is not bad. Destruction comes to us when we remain chained to our past, no matter what characterized it. If we have lived a selfish, obviously sinful life, it is quite simple to see the error in clinging to our old habits and thought patterns. It takes no great mental gyrations to see the futility of holding on to a way of life which brought so much sorrow. But when Jesus said, "Remember Lot's wife," I believe He was speaking also to those women (and men) who cling *unhealthily* to the good and lovely things of the past once these things are gone forever.

No woman ever learns to live again after she has lost her husband in death, if she insists upon clinging to the memory of their happy years together. No woman can forget those years, and she should not. But memory must be held in balance by our enlightened intelligence. There is a life and death difference between holding a memory with gratitude and joy, and remaining chained to it. When we hold a memory gratefully, we move forward. When we clutch it, demanding from it still, we move into unreality and neuroticism and people begin at once to have to tiptoe around our personalities.

God Himself gave Lot's wife a chance to escape the destruction that was falling on Sodom, but she refused to escape. The chain was secured, and by her own hands. Even God could not free her, because she would not be freed.

God Himself wants to provide an escape into freedom for us from grief, hurt feelings, disillusionment, trouble of any kind; but because He has created us with free wills, as He created Lot's wife with a free will, we can block Him by securing the chains of our past lives with our own hands.

When we refuse to move forward, giving our first attention to the future and what lies ahead in God's will for us, we solidify ourselves as surely as Lot's wife was turned into a stationary pillar of salt! Perhaps the thing to which we cling from the past was a blessed and good and helpful thing. Perhaps while it was happening we were enabled to grow from it, to become better persons. But then it is suddenly gone from us. We are not there anymore, not in that place, not with that person, no longer in those circumstances. We are in a new place, or the old place seems new and strange because he or she is no longer there. The old life is changed or finished, a new one must be found or created. The future is fuzzy and black and confusing. The old, dear circumstances seemed so clear, so creative, so comfortable, so right. We have a choice to make here: either we believe God remains the same in these new, strange, frightening circumstances, or we don't. God seemed near before, when that loved one was still where we could see him, and hear his voice, and touch his hand. We felt sure God had made that situation. It was so good, so happy, so glad, only God could have created it! Now it is gone. We are bereft in our today. But has God changed? Is He not able to deliver us out of this dark place into another light place? Not the same old familiar one, but wherever God leads us is the place He has for us, and if He is real and if we know something of His intentions toward us, we will be able to go with Him. The tears may still be streaming down our faces, and our hands may shake, but we will be able to go and not to look back, except to give thanks for what was there for those years or months or days.

Lot's wife looked back toward a wrong thing and clung to it. But the same principle applies. God speaks to us in this Eternal Now, where He has always been and will be forever. God does not move in a stretched out ribbon of time. He moves toward us in the Now. He urges us toward life today.

Without a personal relationship to God in Jesus Christ, I fail to see how anyone ever recaptures the courage or the will to live for today after a great loss. But with Him it is possible for anyone. We cannot "fix" things at once for ourselves, but we can hold the past light, with gratitude, and turn our eyes toward Now where He is waiting with a new day, and we can look ahead to a new tomorrow where He will still be Himself with us, as He was in those days which are gone. Only God can never leave us nor forsake us. And He never will.

3. REBEKAH

A Bundle of Contradictions

It was evening and time for the women to come to the well
for water. A strikingly beautiful young woman was there
with her large clay pitcher, ready to lower it into the well,
when she heard the clop-clop of camels slowing under the
shouts of their drivers. A small but luxurious caravan appeared out of its own cloud of dust, and a man, dignified
by his age and his expensive clothes, dismounted and
walked toward her.

The well was back in Mesopotamia, in Haran, the town
where Abraham's brother, Nahor, still lived with his wife
and children. The traveler was Abraham's faithful old servant, Eliezer, who had prayed over every dusty mile of the
way from Canaan that the Lord God would honor his important mission. He had made an oath with Abraham that
he would find a suitable wife for his beloved Isaac from
among Abraham's own people. But not any wife would do,
and so Eliezer had been specific with the Lord when he
prayed: "See, I am standing here by the well while the
daughters of the townsmen are coming out to draw water.
May it be so, that the girl to whom I say, 'Please, lower
your pitcher so that I may drink,' and who shall answer,
'Drink, and I will water your camels, too,' that she may be
the girl Thou hast designated for Thy servant Isaac. By this
I shall know that Thou has treated my master, Abraham,
graciously."

The dark-eyed young woman watching him walk toward
her caught his attention at once. Among the other women
gathering at the well, she was like a tall, fresh lily standing
in a bed of thistles. He asked for water, and every single
specification of his prayer began to be met: she showed
kindness and courtesy, and the sort of warm-heartedness
gentle Isaac needed in his wife; her physical strength was
extraordinary—she could offer Isaac a strong body to bear
his children and health for sharing long years of married
life. A woman who could draw and carry enough water to

quench the thirst of a caravan of camels was no weakling.
Rebekah met every requirement and more.

*Everything this woman does, she does beyond expecta-
tion,* the old servant mused to himself as he watched her
set down the last empty water pitcher with enough
youthful energy left to run, flushed and even more
beautiful, back to where he waited. She smiled at him, then
threw back her head and laughed in the sheer joy of ac-
complishment.

Before he handed her the most beautiful gold bracelets
and ring she had ever seen, the old man asked cautiously,
wanting each detail to be in order: "Whose daughter are
you? And, please tell me, is there room at your father's
house for us to lodge?" Her answers to these questions
would be his ultimate sign that the Lord God had led him
to this remarkable young woman.

"I am the daughter of Bethuel, the son of Milcah, whom
she bore to Nahor." This much was perfect! Nahor was
Abraham's own brother. To the second question she
replied, welcoming him with her smile: "We have plenty of
straw and fodder and space for you to spend the night."

Eliezer presented her with the bracelets and ring and
began to worship God for prospering his mission, but
Rebekah was too excited to do anything but run to her
father's house to tell everyone everything that had happened and to show them her new jewelry.

Rebekah's brother Laban listened long enough to get the
gist of her story about the rich visitor, then ran outside
toward the well, sensing more possible good fortune in the
arrival of the strange caravan.

"Come in, you blessed of the Lord," he shouted to old
Eliezer. "Why stand outdoors when I have gotten the
house ready, as well as a place for the camels?"

As quickly as possible, a lavish meal was prepared and
set before them—savory kid's meat, vegetables seasoned
with spices, flat round loaves of fresh bread, melons, mul-
berries and honey—but the old man refused to eat until he
had told his story in detail. Laban's sharp, dark eyes
squinted with interest as he listened to the impressive but
seemingly endless account of Abraham's wealth. The story
of the journey to Nahor's town unfolded then, the old
servant savoring every word he spoke.

"My master made me swear that I would secure no wife
for his son from among the daughters of the Canaanites in
whose land he now lives. I was to come here, to the house

of his relatives, and bring back a wife for Isaac who will inherit all his father's wealth."

Rebekah fidgeted on her low stool, her eyes dark with excitement.

Bethuel, the father, started to speak, but Laban had caught on to their guest's passion for detail. *This* guest must have things *his* way! The young man silenced his father: "Go on, honored guest, until you have quite finished."

Slowly, in his deliberate way, the faithful old steward droned on. Rebekah knew the story he was telling now . . . she had been at the well with him; she did wish he'd get to the point. But, he was only as far as the part where he bowed himself to worship God after she had watered his camels and received the gold bracelets and the beautiful ring. The old voice was saying, "I praised the Lord God of my master Abraham, who had guided me in the right road to take the daughter of my master's brother for his son." Rebekah jingled her bracelets in her nervousness. "Now then, if you are going to treat my master kindly and fairly," the old man was saying, "let me know." Once more Bethuel, their father, cleared his throat to speak, but Eliezer wasn't finished. "Or if not, let me know, so I may turn to the right or to the left."

Bethuel then managed his first comment—but not alone; we are told that both Laban and his father replied: "This thing is from the Lord, take her and go . . . !"

Eliezer then clapped his hands and his servants delved into their baggage and brought out lavish gifts for everyone. There was some hesitancy about their leaving the next day—it seemed sudden and almost unceremonious, but Eliezer was eager to get started, so with her nurse, Deborah, Rebekah said good-by to her family and excitedly mounted a camel in the caravan which began to move once more along the road south toward Canaan, where Abraham and Isaac lived.

*   *   *

We have called the story of Rebekah *A Bundle of Contradictions.* To this point, few if any contradictions within this young woman's personality are evident. She seemed to be the perfect wife for Isaac. In every way, old Eliezer's prayer appeared to be answered. As she rode off with the caravan, Abraham's servant could have asked for no more

from the Lord God. The young woman was courteous,
kind, industrious, and like Isaac's mother, Sarah, extremely
beautiful. More than that, the old man was pleased to find
a woman with a mind of her own. Not that the custom of
her day would have given her the chance to refuse, but
Rebekah seemed to know at once that she wanted to go to
Isaac. Eliezer apparently knew Abraham and Isaac well,
and perhaps he understood that Isaac, who was still grieving over Sarah's death, needed a strong-willed woman for a
wife. And watching Rebekah through this beginning of her
story, no one can mistake the similarity between her and
Sarah. Both were opinionated, both intelligent, impetuous,
both extremely beautiful. In fact, Rebekah was extremely
many things.

And just because she has presented only the positive side
of her attractive personality so far in her story, we must
not jump quickly to the conclusion that she has only a
positive side. She will turn out to be a rather striking exam-
ple of what women today still find true of their own personalities, if they take an honest look. In us all are puz-
zling *contradictions*. We may present our best side before
guests, but what about later, when the guests are gone?
What we present then may startle us and fill us with guilt.
But there is a way open to women today for the integration
of the contradictions within their personalities. Jesus Christ
has come, and He is the great integrator. If a woman's personality is under His control, she need not be a victim of
the bundle of contradictions within herself. "We are complete in Him."

As Isaac's Loyal Wife

The long, single line of camels neared the fields around
Abraham's encampment back in Canaan, and Eliezer's
heart swelled with pride and gratitude that he had been so
successful. In fact, he could scarcely wait to tell his
story—in detail, of course—to both Abraham and to Isaac.
Twilight was softening the low hills and the desert stretches
around the camp when the caravan drew close enough for
Rebekah to notice a tall, richly dressed man walking alone
in the fields.

Ignoring her nurse Deborah's admonition, she slid from
her camel to the ground. The man walking in the field had
seen the caravan, and now he was striding toward them, as
though he could no longer contain his excitement. Rebekah

ran along beside a foot servant, "Tell me, who is that man walking through the field to meet us? Who *is* he?"

"That is my master, Isaac, out meditating according to his custom every day."

Isaac! Only the Lord God could have done a thing so marvelous as this. Much more than his manly, almost regal appearance accelerated Rebekah's heart and made it sing words like nobility, respect, reverence—love! She could respect a man like this. She could respect Isaac, and she could *love* him. He was closing the distance between them rapidly now, and Rebekah was glad to see that he was twice as old as she, forty, perhaps.

With a start, Rebekah realized she had been standing with her face uncovered, openly admiring his broad shoulders draped with a blue and gray woolen cloak, his long easy stride, his wide hand shielding his eyes. Could she wait to see those eyes? No choice now, her veil must be lowered, she must appear properly modest.

Isaac hurried up to them, unsmiling at first, looking for her. When he found her, he didn't look away again, even when old Eliezer launched upon his deliberate narrative, complete to every small event. Courteously, Isaac let the old man finish, still looking at Rebekah, his eyes smiling now, as though to say, "Eliezer will be finished eventually, then we can be together."

They were together in the place most sacred to Isaac. He took her at once into Sarah's tent, which he and his father had kept intact as it had been on the day the high-spirited old lady died, at the age of 127. Quite simply we are told that "he came to love her." And that in her, "he found consolation after his mother's death." From the beginning, the marriage of Isaac and Rebekah was much more than an arrangement to please an aging father.

Abraham lived to be 175 years of age, and sired 6 more sons by his second wife, Ketura. There is no record that any confusion or trouble arose among Isaac and his half brothers. No record that Isaac resented Ketura, the woman who took his adored mother Sarah's place in his father's life. Perhaps this is the best indication we have that his marriage with Rebekah was a successful one. She really did help fill the emptiness in Isaac's heart after Sarah's death. It would not be farfetched to imagine that Isaac, who had never been a man of action like his father, Abraham, came rather to depend on Rebekah's energetic judgments. After all, Sarah had pampered Isaac, and since, at forty, he was still grieving over the loss of his mother, it is not unreasonable to believe that he leaned on Rebekah. He could lean on her, because like Sarah, Rebekah seemed to thrive on any situation that challenged her.

For the first twenty years of their life together, Isaac and his beautiful wife shared their thoughts and their hearts. Over and over they were forced to break up their home and move to still another place where there was enough water for Isaac's always increasing flocks and herds, but there is no mention of any grumbling whatever from Rebekah. Not even to her faithful nurse, Deborah, who stayed with her for many years. If Isaac felt they needed to move again, her courage and high spirits made the new adjustment possible. Like her mother-in-law, Sarah, whom she never knew, Rebekah was genuinely devoted to her husband.

Like Sarah, also, Rebekah carried the dark burden of barrenness for all of those first twenty years of her life with Isaac. In this one way only, she felt inadequate. In every other way, she knew herself to be a good wife.

Then, at the end of the first twenty years, God answered Isaac's fervent prayer for a child. We are told that "within her body the children jostled each other." Rebekah was going to bear Isaac not one child, but two! The Lord Himself told her before the twins were born: "Two nations exist in your womb, and two peoples shall separate from your body, one stronger than the other, and the older shall serve the younger."

As the boys, Esau and Jacob, grew to manhood, unlike in every way, they *were* as "two nations"—two warring nations; and with this strife between brothers, came the resultant strife between Rebekah and Isaac. Because Isaac was a quiet man, his extreme devotion to his ribald, red-haired, rugged son, Esau, helped compensate for the fact that he had lived in many ways, around the edges of life. Isaac loved Esau because he was a great hunter, a man of action. Rebekah seemed almost to hate Esau, her firstborn, and turned with all the extreme side of her nature, toward the clever, thoughtful son, Jacob. Rebekah and Isaac no longer shared their hearts. They did not even share their sons. The event which should have strengthened their relationship, began to shatter it!

*   *   *

More marriages than this one—then and now—have

started to crumble with the birth of children. When a woman of Rebekah's unusually strong character becomes a mother, she *can* become a stranger to her husband. In many ways, gentle Isaac had been her "child," and now her only apparent inadequacy was gone forever—she had children of her own. Isaac still needed her in the same old ways, but she felt complete; and at once the narrative begins to mention Isaac's advancing age. The change in his beloved Rebekah made an old man of him.

Perhaps the change began even before Esau and Jacob were born, while they "jostled each other" within her body. With this "jostling" there began the first serious jostling of the contradictions within the personality of Rebekah herself. The one place where she had been weak, vanished: she was no longer barren. The intelligent, strong-willed woman took the reins of all their lives in her own hands and never dropped them again. Where before she had discussed their problems with Isaac, she now began to give orders. Where she had been tender and charming, she grew sharp and cunning. Perhaps she was not aware of this, but even her attitude toward the Lord God must have changed. Rebekah had been devout, but no one who rightly reveres the Lord God takes the reins of her life and the lives of her family into her own hands.

If she ever remembered the tall, gentle man of God whose whole being made her heart sing the first evening she saw him striding toward her across his father's field, she shut the memory from her mind. They didn't quarrel, Isaac loved her too deeply for that; but the emergence of the tryant in Rebekah twisted and distorted all that had been good about the years in which she took Sarah's place in Isaac's heart. Now he was merely a troublesome problem to her. No shred of the once valued respect for him was left. She saw that he was cared for (he had grown ill and old and blind), but he was a burden and an obstacle in her determined new course because he favored Esau, whom she despised.

God had said to her before the twins were born: "Two nations exist in your womb, and two peoples shall separate from your body, one stronger than the other, and the older shall serve the younger." Esau came first, with Jacob clinging to his heel at birth. And God had said, "the older shall serve the younger." Jacob was the younger, and with all her heart, Rebekah wanted to see her beloved Jacob Esau's master! As a result, she forgot or discarded her feeling of affection for her husband in her growing desperation to *make* what God had said to her come true. Surely Isaac would die soon, and she could not tolerate the thought of her boorish son, Esau, as head of their household.

Within us all, there exists the same potentially contradictory traits. They may take years to show up, but they are in us all. A change of circumstances can bring them rioting into action, changing us almost beyond recognition. It is a subtle thing to the person in whom the contradictory forces operate, however. We are quickly self-deceived. Inside we may feel the same as ever. But the safest way to check our personalities for the imbalance of these contradictory forces, is to check the behavior and reactions of those with whom we live. Do they fear us when once we gave them comfort and security? Do they "walk on eggshells" around us, when once there was a sane and comfortable interchange of ideas? Do people have to "handle us with kid gloves" to avoid trouble? Have those near us stopped confiding in us? Is the conversation different at the dinner table? If so, could it be because *we* are different?

A "change" like this is tragically commonplace, when people reach middle life or even before. Within us all are these contradictory forces which must not only be held down or squelched, they must be *integrated*. In short, we must be "pulled together" at the center of our beings, or the loose reins of the wild horses of our natures will fly in all directions, scarring those whom God has given us to love, scarring ourselves.

Only one Hand can hold these reins in check, and this Hand is outstretched toward us all the day long, saying, "Behold Me, behold Me." If your disposition runs riot when you least expect it, behold the Man-God who longs to keep you under His quiet, steady control.

Keep "looking unto Jesus, the author and finisher of our faith."

As Isaac's Contradictory Wife

As a young man, Jacob had delighted Rebekah, his mother, by tricking Esau in a weak moment of animal hunger, into selling him his birthright for a bowl of lentil stew. Technically, at least, now the "older would serve the younger." But this transaction was almost meaningless unless Jacob could somehow get his father to give him the blessing still due Esau the first born.

Obsessed with her desire for Jacob to receive the blessing, Rebekah's alert mind catalogued every scrap of useful information; daily she flattened herself against the sides of Isaac's tent, eavesdropping, sifting every idle and meaningful sentence the old man uttered to his beloved Esau, waiting for the needed opening. One day it came. Isaac asked Esau to go out and kill a deer and prepare his favorite venison dish, so that they could feast and so that he could bestow his blessing upon his first born son. As soon as Esau was safely out of sight toward the hills, Rebekah and Jacob went into action. She prepared a young kid from their flock, as she knew her blind husband preferred it, quickly fastened goat's hair on Jacob's chest and wrists and hands, so that his smooth skin would feel like Esau's hairy hide when the sightless old man touched him, handed him the dish of stew, and offering to take his curse upon herself if things went wrong, sent her favorite son off to *steal* his brother's blessing.

Rebekah, huddled in her tent with her adored Jacob, heard Esau's loud cries of anguish when he and his blind old father discovered what had happened. Isaac had fallen into her trap. It was now Jacob, her slim, intelligent, clever Jacob, who would be the head of their family when her husband died! She gripped Jacob's slender fingers the more tightly. They had done it. Rebekah had what she wanted.

In Isaac's tent, Esau and his father also clung to each other, the big hairy man begging as a child begs, for Isaac to give him some kind of blessing. During the quiet moments that followed, as old Isaac prayed over his son, Rebekah and Jacob waited. His heart crushed with disappointment and his fury raging, Esau left his father's tent after awhile and trudged heavily toward his own. As he walked, the hot grudge burst into words. Unaware that his mother and Jacob were listening, he muttered to himself: "Mourning time for my father is not far off. He will die soon. Then—then I will kill my brother, Jacob. Then I will surely kill him."

Rebekah's mind went into action again, as she began to formulate a new plan. Mother and son stood now some distance apart in her tent, Rebekah unaware of the moment Jacob dropped her hand, trying not to see the strange expression on his handsome face—a young man suddenly cornered, almost ready to run. Her thoughts tumbled wildly for a moment. This new crisis could not be coming between them! Not between *them*. Nothing could ever come between Jacob and his mother.

As her composure began to return, she unfolded her new plan. Jacob would leave at once for her brother Laban's house at Haran. He would be safe there. He would stay for only a short while—just until Esau's anger was forgotten. "Esau is so stupid, he won't be able to keep it for long." Jacob studied her face, as she spoke. "Then I'll send for you and get you back from there, my beloved. Back here with me. If your father is dying, why should I be deprived of you both at once? Don't worry, I'll handle your father. I'll get his permission for you to leave."

She did. As though the old man's heart had not been broken by the deception, early the next morning Rebekah began skilfully to maneuver Sarah's son, Isaac, now so old and weakened by his new pain. "We must take action, Isaac, and right away. The presence of those two vulgar Hittite women Esau married wears me down so constantly, and if Jacob marries one of them, too, my life won't be worth living!"

Not a word passed between them concerning the treachery against him and Esau. Isaac could not argue with her. Tears ran from his empty eyes, so desperately did he long to *look* at his wife, to try to find some familiar sign that she was considering him, too, as in the old days. But he could not see her, nor trust his voice to reply. He could only listen as he had been forced to do now for so long; listen and feel his heart break again because Rebekah had no words of comfort for him, no words of understanding that his pain was enormous at having hurt Esau, whom he loved.

"Isaac, are you listening to me? We must send Jacob away at once—back to my brother Laban's house, to get a wife from among our own people! He will be here in a few minutes now for your blessing on his trip, so sit up."

Rebekah was waiting for Jacob when he left his father's tent. "Tonight my son—you mut leave tonight." Jacob needed no urging, he was ready. He was obeying her, following her plan exactly, but why was he so remote and unruffled at saying goodby?

That night her words flew at him more to comfort herself than Jacob. "You want to come back, don't you, Jacob?" He smiled, but she was not reassured. For the first time she hated his being so clever. He was turning away, her fingers clutching his cloak. "Even though we deceived your father, we were only doing God's will! The Lord Himself told me your ugly brother would serve you."

Jacob kissed her lightly and was already striding away. "I'll send for you, Jacob," she called. "Trust God. What we did was God's will! Be careful, my son. I'll send for you. I'll ... send ... for you."

He was out of sight now into the darkness, with no more waving. Had he changed? Or was this the only way he could go? Could one young man be so tender and so calloused? Esau was always the same—a boor with a boor's heart and brain. Isaac was always the same—no fight in him, too gentle and too weak. What was Jacob really like?

Her desolation now that Jacob was gone, crowded out her questions. Rebekah sobbed, knowing suddenly in her empty heart that she would never see her strange, beloved, perplexing son again.

Knowing, too, that this fine, intelligent, devious young man—this masculine bundle of contradictions, was *her* son.

When he did return many years later, his mother was dead.

*   *   *

I cannot believe Rebekah was a totally cruel woman. She was a woman suddenly under the control of a passion to have her own way. In her time, as now, a certain type of man—Isaac's type of man—gives in to a strong woman like Rebekah, rather than suffer the painful pressure of argument. To please her he had blessed Jacob before he left; what would be accomplished now if he refused? In every outward way, Rebekah got what she wanted. But in the process, she lost all that mattered. Jacob did not come back in her lifetime, and Isaac outlived her.

This woman's reasoning is difficult to follow, mainly I think, because she was not *reasoning*, but moving entirely on her emotions. It is true that God did tell her before her sons were born that the older would serve the younger, a situation directly opposed to custom. Did Rebekah believe she had called on the Lord God to help her in the desperate deception she planned? Did she, as do women today, want this thing so much she rationalized to the extent of believing God would help her bring it off? Did she *think* herself into believing that because of what God had said, she was free to go to any lengths to make this come true? What did God mean by that strange statement implying the shift in the actual birthright of her sons? Did He merely know in advance, as He knows everything, that the trick *would* be brought off? Was He merely stating a fact? Was it in or out of God's will? Once more, Rebekah, and we who live in the twentieth century, cannot always understand *all* of what God says. We attempt to replace Him when we even try. His ways *are* higher than our ways, and He does not expect us to understand His every word; what He expects is that we understand something of the intention of His heart and trust Him with the rest.

No one can be sure which way Rebekah's tormented thinking turned her where God was concerned. One thing we do know—she set her once beautiful face toward treachery in order to capture the prize of the paternal blessing for *her* favorite, Jacob. What happened to Isaac and Esau seemed not to matter. Her energies and high spirits, once so attractive and comforting to Isaac, were poured relentlessly and skillfully into the deception, and she could not be stopped because she *would* not be!

What had been her strength, turned to weakness. What had been her charm, turned to cruelty. Is it surprising that the same contradictory nature in Jacob should have begun to frighten her toward the end? No mother can completely trust her child's heart if she cannot completely trust her own. No woman can do away with the contradictions in her own personality or in the personalities of those she loves. Only God can unify our inner selves, and we, like Rebekah, too often decide to run our lives in compartments. We make use of God when it is convenient, or when it seems to serve our purposes. But we remain compartmentalized: God here, we there. In all fairness, there was some explanation for Rebekah's contradictory life. God was still mainly a remote mystery to her in spite of her faith, but He need not be to us. The fact will remain forever: He has now revealed Himself in Jesus Christ, and He is available to every woman to unify, to integrate her inner contradictions, to redeem her divided self.

4. RACHEL AND LEAH

Two Sisters Who Loved the Same Man

A young shepherdess, her face wind-and sun-browned, sat unself-consciously, half-sprawled like a bored child, under the feathery branches of a tamarisk tree, dreaming. Nothing around her in the fertile, but plain hilly country outside the city of Haran, in northern Mesopotamia, matched her beauty. Even her father, Laban, always loathe to compliment, had been known to admit she was more beautiful than his sister, Rebekah, who had left the humdrum life around Haran years ago, to marry a rich relative named Isaac. More beautiful than Rebekah? This never failed to startle the young girl dreaming now under the tamarisk tree, to startle and rouse her to more active dreaming. Dreaming which always ended with an unladylike kick out there on the hillside where she was alone except for her father's sheep. Up she would jump at a certain point in the familiar pattern of the dream and kick the trunk of her favorite tree! Why didn't a husband like Isaac send for *her*?

She laughed at herself then, and stooped to brush her slender brown fingers over the little scars her sandals had made through the recent months of dreaming and kicking the uncomplaining tree.

"You're a good tree," Rachel spoke aloud alone in the afternoon wind. Why was it so much simpler to love trees and sheep than people? Did she really love anyone yet? Her mother? She shrugged. Her father, Laban? She laughed aloud, not bitterly, merely because this had never occurred to her. She loved his sheep and tended them when they were in the hills near their home, with genuine care. She was a better shepherdess than her plain, nervous, older sister, Leah; this she knew. After all, poor Leah had such weak eyes, their father Laban could only trust her to care for a few sheep at a time—trouble could be on the flock before old squinty Leah even noticed. "No," Rachel decided, "I don't love my father. He's my father, I respect

52

him, but I don't think I love him. Leah? Do I love Leah?"
She dropped that for sheer lack of interest. Anyway, the
sun was dropping down the sky; time to be leading the
sheep back to the water holes. The men would be there
waiting to roll the big rocks off the holes so the sheep
could be watered first and out of the way before the cattle
finished grazing.

She didn't start back at once, though. There were a few
more thoughts to think: Rebekah, her aunt, less beautiful
than she, and yet for all these years away from dreary
Haran, married to a wealthy, handsome prince; while Rachel, the shepherdess, sat day after day under a tamarisk
tree and dreamed.

She stretched and began running lightly toward the flock
of sheep, then slowed to a gliding walk ahead of them, so
as to keep their confidence. In all this time, there had been
only one bit of news of her Aunt Rebekah. After years of
barrenness, she had given birth to twin sons, older than Rachel; one a rough creature, with a red hairy body, the
other, dark and sensitive and clever. They had all supposed
Deborah, the young nurse who went with Rebekah, would
one day return to Haran. Rachel longed for that day. From
Deborah, as old as her aunt now, she could really find out
about Rebekah's life.

Suddenly there was no need to wait for Deborah because
that very evening, beside the same well from which her
aunt had drawn water for old Eliezer's camels, Rachel's
dreary world turned upside down. Jacob himself,
Rebekah's handsome, dark, clever son, although weary
from his long journey, rolled away the huge stone so her
sheep could drink. He fell helplessly in love with her—and
she with him!

After profuse greetings and hospitality, the two young
people slipped away from Laban's family and walked
together back toward the well. The dark young man standing beside her was more than a charming new acquaint-
ance, more than a cousin to be proud of, more than a
welcome visitor: he was a *miracle. It is as though today on
the hillside, I dreamed him into being,* she thought, and
decided to take him to see her scuffed-up tamarisk tree
some day. There would be time now, since he was going to
stay at least a month. She knew by then she would be able
to tell Jacob anything.

The next day impetuous Jacob made his first deal with
his wily uncle Laban. His departure from his father's house

had been so sudden, he had brought no gifts. He would work one full month, giving his expert herdsman services free, to compensate; but after that, the important new agreement went into effect. Laban gave his word that in exchange for seven years of labor among his flocks and herds, Jacob could have Rachel for his wife.

There was joy around the table that night, as Rachel and her family shared their food with Jacob. Joy on every face, that is, except one. Rachel's older sister, Leah, was there, her poor eyes weaker and redder than usual from weeping, for from the first moment she saw him, quiet Leah had loved Jacob, too.

*   *   *

It is not at all extreme to believe that Rachel envied her Aunt Rebekah whom she had never seen. After all, hers was the type personality which craves excitement, romance. Even in the days when most marriages were made for expediency, Rachel dreamed of real love invading her empty, boring life. The very fact of her unusual beauty quite naturally caused her to believe she deserved romance. She operated, as do beautiful women today, on the premise that since everyone considered her lovely, *her* romance should be of the spectacular variety. Unlike her homely sister, Leah, who had no right to expect much, Rachel expected everything from love. And this characterizes her exactly—she did fall deeply in love with Jacob on sight, but Rachel expected *from* love, having never been forced to think of giving *to* love. People were delighted to have Rachel around: "she was lovely of form and face." Her charm and physical beauty drew people to her with little or no effort on her part. Leah long ago had learned that she must earn her way into the hearts of other people. "Leah's eyes had no sparkle" (Berkeley). Whether this meant her eyes were weak and blind, or merely dull and listless, is beside the point. Rachel was the charmer who expected; Leah, the dull one who gave—perhaps not from choice, but at least from necessity. And both women were in love with Rebekah's son, Jacob.

Humanly speaking, we could say "poor Jacob" if we hadn't already discovered the young man's capacity for taking care of himself; if we hadn't already discovered his mother's contradictory nature in him. Humanly speaking, we would simply expect Jacob to be able to handle both women and any ensuing complications. After all, he knew what he wanted as much as Rachel knew. He had already stolen his brother's birthright and blessing, with his mother backing him up every inch of the way. Jacob was well equipped to handle things on the human level.

We must, however, attempt to learn to look at people— Jacob, Rachel and Leah—as well as those with whom we live and work, from God's viewpoint; and God's viewpoint is always objective and in true perspective. If your interest and sympathy run to Rachel, you are also seeing her as God sees her. If you are interested mostly in Jacob and sympathize with him, this is God's viewpoint too! How can that be? Simply because He sees us all with equally intense interest and sympathy. This does not mean He agrees with our concepts or desires, and surely it does not mean that He condones selfish actions on our part; but it does mean He understands them and concerns Himself with our total behavior with intense and equal interest. He is every minute mindful of us in our every predicament, whether it is a self-made predicament, or inflicted from outside ourselves.

Here in the beginning of this fantastic story of tangled human relationships, we must get one thing clear: God is not only interested in our predicaments, He is in them with us, attempting to bring us through them in a vastly improved state—if we permit Him to take control.

Rachel and Jacob apparently did fall deeply in love—at first sight. It requires no stretch of the imagination at all, to realize that poor, lonely Leah loved him, too. The scene is set for real drama. Our sympathies will be stirred and repelled one way and then another as the story unfolds; but for now, one thing must be seen: God is the main Character in the drama, and Leah and Rachel and Jacob are human beings like you and me. He will work with and through them according to how much they begin to understand about love *from His viewpoint*. If we see this here, we may find it simpler to see Him in the same role in our own lives which we are living out bumpily, and then seemingly successfully, and then bumpily—right here in the twentieth century. God *is* involved with us all, and is every minute mindful of the necessity for working out His plan in our lives, as surely as He was mindful of His covenant plan through Jacob.

Another Deliberate Deception

Seven years is a long time for a man to work for the woman he loves, but Jacob did it—surprising perhaps everyone but himself and Rachel, the only two who could have known the depth and quality of their love. Both these self-centered young people were finding in themselves a capacity to love which neither must have recognized fully yet. Rebekah's clever son, Jacob, who had deceived both his father and his brother, was finding in himself the capacity to love as few men ever love. Spoiled, beautiful Rachel was stirring this capacity to life, not only because of her beauty—but because she was Rachel. To Jacob this was enough.

He labored among Laban's flocks and herds—two, five, six years, counting it all gladness because he knew *that day* would come; the seven years would pass, the sun would come up on one morning some day, and after that Rachel could be with him forever. He half forgot that he now possessed both Esau's birthright and his blessing. Only today mattered, and it mattered so much because it would finally become yesterday and would move him one day closer to the moment when he and Rachel would never have to say good-by again.

When it was the last day of the last of the seven years of Jacob's labor, Laban's household grew noisy with activity. Marriage festivities in those days lasted a week, and began with the bride's being led to her groom on the first night in silence and complete darkness.

Jacob paced his quarters alone, waiting. Now, the moments dragged as they had not through all the long years of labor. His mind seemed strangely undisciplined: he thought of Rebekah, his mother, and felt grief that she could not know of his great happiness; he thought of Isaac, his father, and as always when he thought of him, his mind sped to the Lord God. Remembering God brought vividly the memory of the third night of his long journey to Haran, when the Lord had met Jacob in a dream—a meeting about which he had never told anyone, not even Rachel. A dream in which Jacob had become God's man, had received God's blessing on his life, had experienced God's unique love fresh in the face of his own deceit. Would he ever tell anyone about the dream? Would anyone believe him? Would Rachel? Rachel!

Every footstep tripped his heart now. Surely Laban and
the women would be leading Rachel to him *soon*. Was
Leah with her in her quarters? Tall, plain, loyal Leah,
helping, he imagined, as always.

Jacob tried to see outside into the darkness, failed, and
paced his tent again. Any minute, through that darkness
and silence, *she* would be coming to him. Rachel, with her
slender, lovely shoulders and eyes the color of corn
flowers, seeing all the way into his heart . . . Rachel would
be there soon now, her rounded arms circling his neck, her
face fragrant and close enough to kiss and she would never
have to run away from him again.

Suddenly his pacing stopped; he could hear the slow,
definite footsteps of several people approaching his tent
through the thick, silent, moonless night. According to
custom his tent was darkened, too, with no lamp lit. Then
the footsteps stopped outside and after a moment, he heard
one person walk toward him in the darkness.

"Rachel?"

He reached toward the silent, shadowy figure standing
inside his tent now. "Rachel?" Why didn't she run to him
as she always did? Why didn't he take her in his arms as
he had done for every golden moment, they had ever found
to be alone? Neither moved toward the other as the heavy
silence squeezed in upon them. Then he knew the hideous
truth: This woman was not Rachel! It was Leah.

Jacob could only stand there, as did she, saying nothing
during these first moments: moments of shame and
humiliation and fear for Leah. Moments of anger and
disappointment and a swift, unexpected surge of fresh guilt
for Jacob. His thoughts lurched suddenly away from this
place to his father and Esau, sharing the torment of their
first moments of desperation when they learned of the
deception by Jacob and his mother. Laban had tricked him
in exactly the same way!

Shy, pain-filled Leah found her voice first: "I'm sorry,
Jacob. My father acted according to the law instead of his
agreement with you. I am older than Rachel, and according to the law, I am to marry first. I've loved you from
the moment I saw you all those years ago, but I hate
bringing you sorrow. I could only obey my father, Jacob.
Forgive me, and try to be kind to me and let me be kind to
you."

Jacob's old treachery had met its equal in his uncle,
Laban, his own mother's brother. It was Jacob's *old*

treachery now, however. Somehow, since the Lord God had met him in the dream, love had almost entirely replaced treachery in his heart.

Leah was his wife now, not Rachel, and he must go through with the week's festivities, avoiding when possible, her weak, frightened eyes, so full of love for him. He moved woodenly through the days, knowing he must forever be wary of his uncle and never trust him again.

At the end of the week, well on guard against another trick, Jacob and Laban reached a second agreement: Jacob would have to give his expert herdsmanship for seven more years—fourteen in all, but Laban did agree to allow wedding festivities to begin at once for him and Rachel. Jacob would have two wives, Rachel *and* Leah.

*   *   *

There was nothing unusual about this socially, but the two lovers, Rachel and Jacob, began their married life with a far steeper impediment than a mother-in-law in the house! They wanted only to be alone, but now there would be poor Leah—as much his wife as Rachel, except in Jacob's heart. Perhaps, if—as was so often the case—he had loved neither woman, but only enjoyed their company and welcomed their children, his way might have been simpler.

For our purposes here, however, the deception by Laban is the important thing. Was this God's way of punishing Jacob for his deception of his own father and brother? I think not. God had met Jacob in the dream on his way from his parents' home to Haran all those years ago. When God meets a man as He met Jacob that night, forgiveness takes place. And once God has forgiven, He never punishes for the sin again. Unless we remember this, all our concepts of God become twisted and distorted. The very fact that Jacob made the best of this awkward, painful situation, proves to me that inwardly he had begun to change after his meeting with the God of his father, Isaac. This God had now become the God of Jacob, too. I have heard it said that if He could be the God of Jacob, He could be the God of anyone! This is true, but when He becomes the Lord of the human heart, change has to begin to take place. In Jacob, as in us, it does not happen overnight. Jacob was becoming God's man, as we are always in the process of becoming God's women. This fact, well learned, does away with all our static notions that anyone ever becomes a perfect saint on this earth.

Rachel and Leah were in a difficult predicament—made more difficult for them both because they both truly loved this man—but because Jacob had met God personally before he reached Haran, their chances for a successful life, even under such strange circumstances, greatly improved.

As I see it, God was definitely not punishing Jacob through Laban's trickery. Would the God who *is* love prompt a man to treachery? Does this make sense? No. God was being realistic, as He always is, in allowing the deception. He never stops a man's hand in mid-air. But He never fails to make creative use of even an act of treachery, *if* even one person involved is His follower. In Jacob's case, this enormous heartbreak could be used to teach Jacob how to live in the midst of trouble. The old adage holds here: "All lessons worth learning are learned the hard way." Laban's deceit gave Jacob a chance to learn balance as nothing else could have done.

This does not mean that he began to love both women and suddenly became glad of the deception. He must have suffered constantly in Leah's presence, hating her humiliation, at times disliking himself for wishing he could spend full time with Rachel, pitying Leah. And pity in a marriage relationship can be deadly. Pity incites scorn, indifference, self-defense. There must have been times when, because he found excuses to spend his leisure hours with Rachel, Jacob even felt false guilt. He was becoming God's man, but he was also human.

Rachel had probably never particularly loved her sister, anyway. She couldn't have felt out and out jealousy, Leah was too unattractive; her father was to blame for the difficult situation, not Leah. Rachel most likely was not jealous of Leah as a woman—not at first, anyway, but she must have resented her, despised her, merely for being alive and in the way.

And Leah? Perhaps there is no greater pain than to love as she loved Jacob, and to know she was not wanted. Each time Jacob paid any attention to Leah, she knew he did it because he was forced to. I imagine the only thing that preserved Leah's sanity was the fact that she had learned because of her unattractiveness, to *give* instead of to *expect*. This is creative. Creative giving on Leah's part battled with creative beauty and the ability to give pleasure which

Rachel possessed fully. We must not think off balance here: Rachel's love was real, too. Real and creative. But her natural beauty had made her more a receiver, less a giver. I doubt that Leah knew how to receive. Both qualities are needed for a balanced personality.

Three people never started life together against greater odds, but God was in it with them, never forcing issues, never hurrying their growth: He was simply there with them, totally involved—as He is totally involved today with us, in our every human relationship tangle.

The Spirit of Competition

As the years passed, Rachel held Jacob's heart and his love, and Leah bore his children: Reuben, Simeon, Levi and Judah. Each time Leah bore him a son, she thanked God because now, she thought, Jacob would notice her as a woman. He was pleased with his sons—but Jacob was only at home with Rachel, and his sensitive nature suffered with her because she had borne him no children. Still, his pride in his sons by Leah caused inevitable conflict in him, and one evening, when he had hurried in from the fields to be with Rachel, her mood disturbed him.

"I'm not good company tonight, Jacob—you'll find me more attractive if you spend the evening with my lovely sister, Leah!" Her sarcasm darkened her usually light, gentle eyes, as she walked restlessly back and forth in front of Jacob.

"Did you quarrel with Leah today?"

"Quarrel?" She whirled to face him, her hands on her hips. "We never quarrel—I wish she would quarrel with me. She just sits there with those sick eyes of hers looking at me as though I've done her some great wrong just by being born! But she's sitting there with another one of your children in her arms and—Oh, Jacob, Jacob!"

She flung herself into his arms and held his head down hard against her cheek. "Give me a child, Jacob—give me a child, or I'll die!"

His heart had been torn once too often, and he shouted at her, out of his helplessness, suddenly enraged: "Am I to take God's place? Who has deprived you of fertility? Have I?"

Rachel slipped like a punished child to the floor, and Jacob's heart melted more quickly than his anger had flared. "Rachel . . . don't you know how much I want your child? I love my sons by Leah, but I don't love their mother—you're the one I love, Rachel. You!"

She sprang to her feet, wiping her wet eyes with the backs of her hands. "Jacob, consider my maid, Bilhah; go in to her, Jacob, and let her bear for me."

Bilhah bore Jacob a son, whom Rachel named Dan, thanking God for the boy. It was not her own son, except legally, because she owned her maid, but some of her pain was lessened. When Bilhah bore Jacob a second son, Rachel laughed with joy, making a cruel children's joke with Jacob: "I am going to name this son of ours Naphtali, Jacob, because that means *obtained by wrestling*." Her beautiful eyes sparked fire as she held the second child out to Jacob. "With mighty wrestlings I have wrestled with my sister, Leah, and I have won out!"

This time Rachel forgot to thank God, and Jacob loved her too much to remind her that all the wrestling had been on her side. Leah just went on being Leah, apparently contenting herself with the fact that it was she who had personally borne Jacob his first four sons.

*   *   *

One point comes clear here: the spirit of unhealthy competition had taken possession of Rachel. When competition takes over, it always smothers gratitude. If Rachel had thanked God again, as she did when Dan was born, she might have avoided the temptation to gloat over Naphtali. And, if this temptation had been avoided, quiet Leah might not have taken her first competitive step. Until Rachel gave her maid to Jacob, Leah obviously had never thought of doing the same thing.

Women in the days of Rachel and Leah, and women now, bring out surprising behavior in one another. Did Rachel drive her to it, or is this laying too much blame on Rachel in the face of her own barrenness? Did Leah give Jacob her maid, Zilpah, in order to even the score with Rachel, or because in her simple heart, she didn't want to leave a stone unturned if turning another might give Jacob more joy? True, she had not borne him a son for some time, but whatever her reason, the competitive battle of wits between the two sisters went on, and Zilpah, Leah's maid, bore Jacob two sons also.

Bearing children, when they are wanted, as Jacob wanted sons, is a good thing in itself. But, as with any good thing, when the spirit of unhealthy competition enters the picture, trouble results. If we are under God's control, spiteful competition becomes simply unnecessary to us. It always implies that we are in the driver's seat, attempting to make things work our way. When we truly follow God's leading, the responsibility of either our failures or successes falls on God, and we can accept either with quiet hearts, knowing He is in charge.

Rachel's Heart Is Changed

Leah bore Jacob two more sons and a daughter, and then, at last, his beloved Rachel, herself, bore him a beautiful son, Joseph. Her own comment, as she held this man-child who was to grow into the most Christ-like man in the Old Testament story, was unlike the impetuous, strong-willed, competitive Rachel: "Now," she said simply, "God has taken away my reproach."

Jacob had matured into a successful, balanced man. He had made a resonably good life in spite of the prickly human tangle between his two wives who loved him so much. His uncle Laban had managed to grow rich at the hands of Jacob, and although it appears now that Jacob was truly God's man, he faced the necessity to break with Laban, in order to fulfill his own responsibilities—not only to the Lord God, whom Laban did not follow, but to his growing family. And here, the trouble between Rachel and Leah began to resolve. Jacob spoke in confidence to both women, explaining his desire to leave their father. For the first time, the sisters were united against their father and agreed gladly to go with Jacob.

"What share or legacy is there left us in our father's house? Does he not consider us outsiders? For he sold us and has enjoyed the profits of our dowry as well. For all the wealth God has taken away from father belongs to us and to our children. Now then, Jacob," both women said, "you do whatever God has told you to do."

While Laban was away shearing sheep, Jacob and his two wives and eleven children, and his herds, flocks and servants, started back to his homeland in Canaan. Laban caught up with them, but God gave Jacob His wisdom in the encounter, and at last they said good-by to Laban and never saw him again.

As their caravan wound toward Canaan, Jacob's old guilt and fear of Esau returned. How would his brother receive him after what he had done? When old Deborah, Rebekah's nurse, returned to Haran, bringing the news that Jacob's mother had died long before his father, Isaac, Jacob suddenly must have felt the entire weight of both their guilt, his mother's along with his own. Perhaps his faith in God wavered, was dimmed by the return to the familiar surroundings so full of the memories of his treachery. He grew so afraid of Esau's wrath that he took special precautions for his family. With the aid of his servants, he placed Leah and her children in a safe position in the caravan, and his beloved Rachel and her son, Joseph, in the rear—the safest place of all.

Left alone, to wait for the morning, when they would surely approach Esau's encampment, God took charge of Jacob and gave him, not only a new name, Israel, but the beginning of new courage. In still another personal meeting with the Lord God, Jacob (now Israel) wrestled with Him until his courage rose high enough to demand the blessing he needed so desperately now.

When they met Esau and his families and servants the next day, Jacob's fear was diminished, but didn't vanish entirely until Esau acted in a most surprising way. Instead of violence, as Jacob had a right to expect, the big, short-memoried man threw his arms around Jacob and urged him to join his people so that they could travel and work together!

Jacob knew this was not wise, but the brothers parted friends, and Rachel's husband was in possession not of new human courage, but of a deepened concept of God's love for them all. The kind of deepened concept that fortifies a human heart for more tragedy.

The tragedy which God knew was up ahead, found Jacob enabled to live through it. En route to Canaan, Rachel was once more pregnant. The thought of another child from Rachel, herself, drew Jacob still closer to the heart of God and filled his heart with joy. But on their way, Jacob was forced to watch his beloved Rachel die, giving birth to their second child, Benjamin.

*   *   *

Without a doubt, Rachel died with a changed heart, a heart turned toward the God of Abraham and Isaac, not the household gods of her own father, Laban. She had stolen Laban's gods when they left, and it is not too farfetched to believe that she took them in a last desperate attempt to turn her father toward the God of Israel. So great was her joy when Joseph was born, that her heart simply could not remain competitive and jealous. True, she had given Jacob only one child then, but Joseph was not an average boy; he was born, late in Rachel's life, literally from the mystery of the greatness of the love between his father and mother. Rachel had become God's woman, too, and it was then simple for her to move as one person with her sister, Leah, as they left their father's house with the man they both loved.

Rachel had thanked God when her maid gave birth to Dan, but that was more a self-centered thankfulness, because she had found a way to compete with Leah. When Joseph came, she was overcome with the kind of wonder that turned her heart to true gratitude. God had used her deep love for Jacob, so that when she gave birth to his child, her own heart opened to the Lord God Himself.

So deep was the inroad God had made into Jacob's heart, that his crushing grief at Rachel's death did not turn him against Leah. Without God it would have been easy for him to begin to despise the plain, unattractive woman who was left to him, when he buried his beautiful wife, Rachel, just outside the city of Bethlehem. As He is willing to do in the face of every human heartbreak, God gave Jacob a kind of joy experienced only by those who know Him well. The grief-stricken man was even able to disobey Rachel's last wish, filled as he was at that moment, with the very insight of God Himself! Rachel died weeping, hating so to leave her husband and children. "Call his name Ben-oni, Jacob!" she had pleaded, so great was her grief at leaving them.

"No, my beloved Rachel—Ben-oni means 'child of sorrow.' I must call him Benjamin—'child of happiness'—because you will always mean all happiness to me."

God had given him the beautiful years with Rachel, and God had given him His own insight into that dark moment when she was leaving him. Insight that saw through to the Light on the other side. Light still dim to Jacob, but there, just the same.

Leah lived out her years in faithful loyalty to the man she loved. Little is told us about her after that, but knowing Leah now, we can easily imagine that she doubled her efforts to care for Jacob and his children. From Leah's son

Judah, came the tribe of Judah, and Boaz, Jesse and David. From David's line came Jesus of Nazareth, the Son of God.

At no time did God wave a magic wand and remedy the rough places in the relationship among these three people, but as is His custom, He did work in the mainstream of their lives, gently, relentlessly, bringing each one to the place of maturity where genuine adjustment became possible.

To the end of his long life, Jacob (Israel) did not forget Rachel. Joseph, her firstborn son, became his favorite among his twelve sons. I am certain Jacob came to love and depend on Leah, but there is a valuable truth here for us all today: God never expects the impossible of us. It would have been impossible for Jacob not to grieve for Rachel. Loving her as he did, it would have been impossible for him ever to have forgotten her; to have stopped missing her warmth, her laughter, her beauty. God did not expect this of him. He does not expect it of us. He promises, however, to give us the power to adjust to our heartaches, by being with us forever—*in them.*

5. POTIPHAR'S WIFE

A Woman With an Empty Life

Rachel's son, Joseph, was sold by his jealous brothers into slavery, and brought down into Egypt, where he was purchased by Potiphar, a wealthy and influential courtier of the Pharaoh. In no way was Joseph an ordinary young man. He was so responsible and devout, that his master, Potiphar, grew still more wealthy, because God honored Joseph's presence in his household. He was so mentally alert and wise for his years, Potiphar soon put him in full charge of his household: "He (Potiphar) committed everything to Joseph's care; he did not bother about anything; he simply ate his meals."

Joseph was also the handsomest and most attractive man Potiphar's sensual Egyptian wife had ever seen.

The capable young overseer moved quickly from one duty to another through his busy days in Potiphar's elaborate household. He was in charge of the stables and harness rooms, the rows of wooden chariot shelters; he supervised the other servants and their quarters, the agricultural activities of the enormous estate, and the management of the huge system of granary bins were Joseph's responsibilities. He also was in complete charge of Potiphar's big house and its staff of servants and slaves.

Lolling through her aimless days, Potiphar's beautiful wife found often ridiculous reasons to keep Joseph inside the block of high rooms that surrounded the main lower room and inner garden court. Her life was totally luxurious and totally empty of meaning—until Joseph appeared. From the moment she saw him, she focused her pent-up energies on seducing him. At first, she merely began to show interest in the management of her household—for the first time. Joseph ignored her, except to show her respect, as his mistress. Potiphar's wife was annoyed. She would have to be more definite, she supposed, with this tantalizing man, whose broad shoulders, thick, luxuriant hair and handsome smooth-shaven face, haunted her nights as well as her days.

One day she sent for him, ordering him to stand still,

while she slowly got up from the couch where she lay and walked toward him.

Joseph stood motionless, his eyes looking just above the woman's dark head. The sun caught in her heavy gold earrings, and shot little lights off her jeweled headband into Joseph's averted eyes. She stopped only a few inches from him, her ringed hands barely touching the ornamental girdle around her waist. Joseph looked down at her, in spite of himself, and his blood raced, faster than when he used to run after his father's flocks on a sunny day.

"Joseph," she said huskily, "embrace me—now."

Not one muscle moved in his solemn young face.

"I command you, Joseph—embrace me! We are alone. Who will know? Who will care, for that matter?"

The woman slipped one slim arm around his neck, and her costly perfume crashed against his senses. But he did not move, and now he was looking above her again: "Look here!" he said firmly. "My master does not bother with anything in the house. He has put me in charge of everything. No one in the house is superior to me. He has kept nothing from me except you, because you are his wife. How could I commit so great a crime and sin against God?"

Her heavily painted eyes narrowed, and she backed away—this time. But day followed day and sometime during the passing of every day, she managed to find him alone. The determined woman commanded, cajoled, persuaded, wept. Joseph stood silent before her, serious and relentless in his refusal; and with every show of inner strength on his part, her desire for this strangely honorable young man grew, and the day came when she found him alone in the house, with the other servants safely outside. This time she did not try persuasion, but leaped, like a glorious animal, clutching his cloak, demanding that he obey her. Joseph moved quickly, too, without a word. Not toward her—away, and ran from the house, leaving his cloak in her hands. Her angry, shrill screams brought servants running and in no time, not only the entire household, but Potiphar himself, knew her story.

"That Hebrew slave you brought in to us came to my room to molest me! But when I raised my voice and screamed, he left his coat with me and ran outdoors!"

Potiphar threw Joseph in prison for a time, and nothing more was written about the glamorous woman who could not break his inner strength.

*   *   *

Joseph's inner strength came from the God of his father, Jacob, and his grandfather, Isaac. The boy had been well taught. After all, Joseph was Jacob's remaining joy, after Rachel died, and undoubtedly he spent more time with his father than did the other sons. There must have been a bond between them, as deep in its way, and as mysterious in its constancy as the love between Jacob and Rachel. It is surely admirable, but not at all surprising that Joseph knew how to call on the very strength of God in the face of his tormenting temptress in Egypt.

It seems to me we need to concentrate here on Potiphar's wife, herself. My pity goes toward her, not Joseph, and I can see nothing shocking or surprising in her conduct. Certainly, it did not shock or surprise God. He knew her as she was. And God, regardless of how often His people fail to remember, never forgets that *anyone* who does not know Him personally, is capable of any moral deviation!

We waste an enormous amount of time and energy condemning and clicking our tongues at women like Potiphar's wife. In no sense do I mean to imply that she was not wrong in what she attempted to do—this is scarcely the point. Much can be learned from Joseph's behavior, but much can be learned by seeing that we must make every effort to be realistic about a woman like this.

In the first place, her life *was* empty. She was bored, most likely neglected by her luxury-loving husband. "Potiphar did not bother about *anything*; he simply ate his meals." Her husband was quite obviously more interested in his own stomach than in his wife. Up to this point, her desire for Joseph is certainly understandable and explainable. She had servants to bathe her, to dress her, to prepare her meals, to care for her house. There is no Biblical mention that she had children. Even if she did, they would have been cared for by nurses. The woman had no work at all—nothing whatever to do with her time and energies. As she saw it, she had nothing whatever to offer but herself. She was lonely, frustrated, and must have felt a failure.

Does this make her behavior toward Joseph right? A ridiculous question, of course. But it does explain it, and it should do away utterly with any possible surprise at her actions.

Any shock should be dispensed with as easily when we take our realistic thinking one important step farther: this woman did *not* know Joseph's God. And anyone who does not know Him, is likely to behave in any number of wrong ways. Potiphar's wife was not so much immoral as amoral. Most likely there was nothing in her religious background that would have given her any clue that this was sinful. Even if there had been a set of moral standards in her training, she had no supernatural power on which to draw as Joseph had.

This is our clue: we must make our appraisals (never judgments) strictly on whether or not the person being appraised knows the living God, as we know Him in Jesus Christ. Have you wasted energy and time pondering the behavior of someone (however wrong it may be) knowing full well that person does not know Jesus Christ? If he doesn't know Him, how could he be expected to act as though he does? When we expect persons to act like Christians, knowing full well they are *not,* we do make the cross of Christ "much ado about nothing."

Christians are the last people who should even be *able* to condemn, providing they understand anything at all about the real reason Jesus had to die.

6. JOCHEBED

Mother of Moses

Some thirty-three centuries ago, probably near Memphis, in northeastern Egypt, Jochebed, a devout, quiet Hebrew woman, gave birth to a baby named Moses. Even from a human standpoint, her heritage was a holy one. She was the daughter of Levi, whose descendants were charged with the care of the sanctuary of God. Her husband, Amram, grandson of Levi, son of Jacob, joined her in his own strong faith in the God of Israel. Both were born into Egyptian slavery, but both remained set apart and free in their inner selves with the freedom of unwavering faith.

When the baby Moses was born, Jochebed already had two children, Aaron and Miriam, born also into the burdened existence of slaves to the Pharaoh of Egypt. But at least their young lives had not been threatened, as was the baby Moses' life. Just before Moses was born, the dread decree had fallen from the lips of the Pharaoh: Every male child born to a Hebrew family must be killed at birth!

Jochebed slept at night with the screams and agonized cries of mothers torturing her mind. For months, seldom a day had passed that one or more Hebrew baby boys had not been jerked from a mother's arms and murdered, often before her eyes. Somehow, Jochebed, whose faith drew on the very wisdom of God Himself, had managed to keep little Moses hidden and alive. No one knows exactly where she hid him, the donkey stable, or her storage room piled with clay jars filled with onions, peppercorns, grain, bread and dates; but he was alive at three months, and Jochebed's God-given wisdom was called into use. Some of her household chores must have been neglected, or left to her precocious seven-year-old daughter, Miriam, because the baby's mother worked night and day weaving a basket of bulrushes from the long, sturdy, pliant stems of the papyrus plant.

Little Miriam watched her mother by the hour.

"These rushes are in themselves a protection against

crocodiles, Miriam. God expects us to use our heads even
as we trust our loved ones to His care."

"Are you really going to float the baby on the water in
that basket, Mother?" Miriam stayed keyed to a high pitch
of excitement as she watched Jochebed's deft fingers twist-
ing and fastening the rushes into place.

"Once I plaster it inside and out with pitch,
Miriam—pitch and then clay—it will be water-tight. We
will put Moses inside, and then your part in our plan
begins!"

Over and over Jochebed explained the plan to Miriam,
and each time Miriam's blood tingled and raced around her
slim little body.

"I am going to stand watch along the bank, hidden in
the tall rushes and flowers along the river bank and watch
the baby. This is my job—all mine! And then—" Miriam's
excitement almost choked her when, even in her thoughts,
the big moment came: the Pharaoh's daughter would come
to bathe and see the baby in his homemade crib!

"You know what you are to do then, Miriam?" Her
mother's voice was quiet and steady, readying her small
daughter for the moment when the princess actually saw
her tiny son in his basket.

"Yes, Mother, I know—I know."

The child did know, and remembered Jochebed's teaching well. No one knows how long Miriam had to stand,
stock still, waiting breathlessly, half-hidden in the tall
flowering flags along the Nile River; but the moment
came. The princess and her maids arrived for her daily
bath in the river, and when they found the baby, seven-
year-old Miriam was more than equal to the occasion. The
baby Moses was crying lustily, and Pharaoh's daughter
pitied him: "This is one of the Hebrew's children!"

Suddenly out of the rushes appeared Miriam, poised and
ready. "Shall I go and invite a nurse from the Hebrew
women to care for the child for you?"

"Go!" the princess said.

Miriam ran faster than she had ever run before, to the
spot farther back from the river where her mother had
been waiting, and as they stood before the princess, she
said: "Take along this child and nurse him for me and I
will pay your wages."

Their plan had worked. Their baby was safe now, and
under the care of his own mother, Jochebed. He would
have all the advantages of a young Egyptian prince in the

Pharaoh's own court, but most important of all, during his
formative years, he would be taught by his wise, faith-filled
mother, Jochebed.

*   *   *

Jochebed's name is only mentioned twice in the entire
Bible, but thirty-three hundred years after her death, she is
still remembered as one of the great mothers of all history.

A mother can do nothing higher than instill her own
wisdom and faith and character into her children. In
Moses, in Aaron and in her daughter, Miriam, Jochebed
did just this. A truly creative mother must be an authentic
teacher. Jochebed had taught Miriam well. The seven-year-
old Hebrew slave child conducted herself with amazing
maturity and poise before the Pharaoh's daughter. And
when she ran to get her mother to act as the baby's nurse,
she must have remained poised, giving no sign that she was
the woman's own daughter, or that Moses was her own
baby brother. This clues us into Miriam's innate strength
and balance; but Jochebed had been her teacher, the little
girl, the teachable pupil.

It seems to me that no one should be surprised at Moses,
Aaron and Miriam—all three outstanding human beings.
Look at their mother! And the more we study Jochebed,
the more evident it becomes that mothers mark their children one way or another. She made full, creative use of her
imagination, as well as her practical mind, when she did
not stop with merely frantic prayers to the Lord God to
save her baby, Moses. She was poised even in the face of
potential tragedy; she was able to quiet her inner turmoil
and *think clearly*. The plan she devised was clever, highly
imaginative—and she worked with her hands to bring it to
a successful ending. Jochebed was an authentic woman of
God, balanced, mature, self-controlled. Her emotions ran
deep, but she was not a victim of those emotions. God was
her Master, therefore she was master of herself.

This simple, faith-filled woman trusted her little girl, too.
She taught Miriam patiently, but when the crisis came, she
dared to trust the child to carry out her teaching. She had
taught Miriam to pray also, and to believe God loved His
people. When the long hours of waiting on the river bank
stretched before the small girl, her mother trusted her to
pray for help and wisdom and quiet in her heart.

Jochebed respected the human dignity of her children,

and their lives mirrored her respect. We do not know how long she lived—perhaps she did not live to see her son, Moses, lead his people out of bondage, aided by Miriam and her older son, Aaron. She may not have been among the singers led by Miriam the day God held back the Sea so that the Hebrew slaves could hurry to freedom. But Jochebed's death is unimportant. Her life is what matters, and it was lived to the hilt—not sensationally, but its good effects reach us today, teaching us that a woman under God's control is a woman living her life to its highest and fullest.

7. MIRIAM

Unmarried and Fulfilled

Miriam and her mother, Jochebed, were friends. The influence of Jochebed's friendship lasted for all of Miriam's long, useful and adventure-filled life.

Nothing is recorded about Miriam's activities during the years in which her brother, Moses, lived as an Egyptian prince in the Pharaoh's palace, nor during the forty years in which he lived as a shepherd in Midian. Nothing definite is known about Miriam after Moses' return to Egypt, filled with the holy determination of God Himself to free His people from bondage. But knowing Miriam, even as it was possible to know her as a child of seven, one can be sure her life was creative and busy. Without a doubt, Miriam kept busy ministering to her oppressed people, counseling with Moses and Aaron on their next move. The woman was a patriot through and through—the first woman patriot mentioned in the Bible, in fact. With all her intense energy and intelligence and finesse—a finesse evident even as a small girl—Miriam was a true nationalist. She loved Israel and through all the years of Egyptian oppression, she burned with pride in her heritage, and her zeal seemed only to grow as the years passed.

Miriam loved God, the God of Abraham, Isaac and Jacob. She believed in Him; took Him literally at His promise to protect and make a great nation of the Hebrew people.

Miriam was a prophetess of God, and in the Hebrew language "prophetess" means a woman inspired and directed to teach the will of God. Miriam could teach because she had been well taught under her mother, Jochebed. So, she must have been revered, not only as the sister of their leaders, Moses and Aaron, but in her own right. The prophet Micah spoke of this period, giving equal credit to Miriam as to her famous brothers: "For I brought

74

thee up out of the land of Egypt, and redeemed thee out of the house of servants; and I sent before thee Moses, Aaron and Miriam" (Micah 6:4).

On the glorious day when God at last brought His people through the Red Sea to freedom, it was Miriam who led them in the first national anthem. When the raging waters closed over the pursuing troops of the Pharaoh, up and down the shore on the other side of the Sea, Miriam danced and banged her tambourine with her strong brown hand, her full-throated voice raised in a primitive song of praise to the Lord God. "Sing ye to the Lord, for He hath triumphed gloriously; the horse and his rider He hath thrown into the sea!" Miriam sang and the people sang with her, because they were free, but also because Miriam had that spirit within her which caused people to follow.

Miriam's mother, Jochebed, may or may not have been among the singers responding to Miriam's fire that night, but her spirit was there, alive and contagious in this singular, forceful sister of Moses and Aaron.

But Miriam, the first woman patriot and the first woman singer on record in the Bible, was also a human being with human faults and weaknesses. Sometime after the crossing of the Red Sea, Miriam experienced a genuine spiritual fall. Miriam, the leader, now began to lead in jealousy and bitterness against her own beloved brother, Moses, who had annoyed his sister by marrying a woman of Cush. Not only did Miriam speak publicly against Moses, stirring the people against him but she began to use her strong personality to influence Aaron, too. God Himself took charge, and filled Moses' heart with still more of His love in order to counteract the acid of Miriam's wrath. She had become leprous in her resentment and hatred, and her gentle brother, Moses, healed her, restoring not only her health, but her clear, balanced faith in God.

And the people of Israel proved their respect and devotion to her, by refusing to move on in their journey toward the Promised Land, until Miriam had spent her seven days of leprous exile and had been returned to them.

Like Moses and Aaron, Miriam died before her people had reached the Promised Land, but Hebrew tradition tells us that her funeral was celebrated in the most solemn and reverent manner for thirty days. She died without ever knowing husband or children, in the Wilderness of Zin, near Hebron.

* * *

Perhaps the spiritual fall of this otherwise gallantly spiritual woman can be traced to her unmarried state. At least, it could be considered an effect of it.

I doubt, however, that Miriam was *only* jealous that Moses had a marriage partner when she did not. I don't think she was as simple as this. Miriam was a complex woman with unusually complex abilities and character traits. She may have been Moses' ugly duckling sister, but there is no grounds for this assumption in my opinion, and I doubt that her lack of beauty kept her single.

As I see Miriam, she was a woman with a cause so much greater than her own personal needs that she simply had no time for marriage. While the patriarchs certainly considered the opinions of their wives in their times of decision, women in Miriam's time were just not usually career women. Miriam *was* a career woman. The new nation of Israel, promised by God in His covenant with her ancestors, filled her horizons. From her mother, Jochebed, she caught the strange importance of her baby brother Moses' life, and stood by nobly to help save him when she was only seven. She stood by Moses and Aaron giving them her loyalty and her counsel during the years in which Moses pleaded with the Pharaoh to let his people go. Israel and its destiny filled Miriam's mind and heart and days. Doesn't it make sense that when Moses was married a second time and to a non-believer, Miriam would be tempted to react as she did? She was jealous, yes, but of Moses' time and energies. Israel needed Moses. She was willing to remain single in order to give her entire life to the cause of her beloved country, why couldn't her brother do the same?

All this is speculation, but it stands up under the impact of the poured-out life of this woman. The problem here, however, is not that she was right to remain single, nor that Moses was right to marry again. God was moving His redemptive plan ahead just the same in the face of both their behavior patterns. The problem here was Miriam's utterly human collapse when she had always been so strong: whatever the reason, she simply humanly lost her balance and moved in anger and resentment toward her brother. For a moment, Jochebed's daughter did what her mother did not do in the face of her own emotional turmoil—she lost control. But Jochebed's teaching saved the situation. Their mother had taught all three of her children to *believe* God. Moses was able to come to his sister's rescue with the love of God pouring from his heart toward her. Evidently Aaron righted himself, too. Certainly, ultimately, so did Miriam. There is no more mention of friction or spiritual ambivalence in her life. She lived out the remainder of her years, as any single woman can do—creatively, fruitfully, interestingly, with no sign of any more rebellion of any kind.

Actually, the one dark, tormented period of Miriam's life was so thoroughly touched with the redemptive love of God that far from scarring her life, she allowed God to enhance it! Perhaps no one asked Miriam's hand in marriage, perhaps she was not attractive; surely, the Bible gives no inference that she was ever married. But she gathered all the incompleteness of her years—her loneliness, her childlessness, her resentment, into a redemptive song of praise and service to the God she loved and who can speak now to every lonely woman who will ever bemoan her lot. Miriam has earned her right to remind us that an unmarried woman *can* live creatively and fully because, as she sang that day on the freedom side of the Red Sea, "He hath triumphed gloriously."

Where God is central, creativity *must* be, because He is the Creator God.

8. RAHAB

A Harlot Turned Believer

Rahab, the harlot, checked the long, thick red cord swinging slowly in the hot evening wind, its knotted end dangling free from the window of her house in Jericho. Rahab was beautiful and well-known in the city, popular with the men who stopped regularly with the caravans, and with the men of Jericho. Everyone knew her house, built of sun-dried brick over the gap between the two thick city walls; and her laughter and wine and her ability to spin a yarn, were as well known as her house.

Every day for weeks now, she had checked the heavy scarlet homespun cord. It must have no frayed spot, it must be securely fastened to the house, it must be strong enough to hold the weight of every member of her beloved family. This would be their means of escape when at last the Israelites, camped now on the eastern edge of Jericho at Gilgal, attacked and captured the city.

That they would take Jericho, Rahab had no doubt. She was only waiting. So were the other citizens of Jericho, but they waited in open panic or bravado or hid fearfully in their houses. Even the strong men who drank in her tavern, trembled through their loud talk and curses. And as the days went by, Rahab had stopped reminding them that it was not the men of Israel they feared, but the God of those men.

"God? What do you know of their God, woman?"

"For sure, what does a woman like you know about any god?"

The rough men laughed and failed even to irritate Rahab. A quiet had taken possession of this woman whose life had been spent in selling her wine and her laughter to these men who spent their money and their idle hours in her establishment. Always before Rahab would have had a ribald answer for them. Not now. The new quiet held her and she answered them with silence. After all, she had promised the two spies from Israel, Salmon and Caleb, that if they would promise her safety for herself and her family, she would keep the secret of their upcoming attack.

For years, Rahab had heard of the miracle of the parted waters of the Red Sea, as the Israelites' God led His people to safety on the other side. Everyone had heard the tale, but Rahab believed it. The day she had hidden Caleb and Salmon in the heap of long flax drying on the flat roof of her house, she had said with such clarity and knowledge that both men believed her: "I know that the Lord has given you this country, that the fear of you has come upon us, and that all the inhabitants of the land melt with terror because of you. No one is confident against you any longer, because the Lord your God is God in the heavens above and on the earth beneath."

So Rahab checked the thick cord every day—and waited. She had lied to protect the two Israelite spies the day they came to look over the city from the vantage point of her house on the wall; but she did protect them, and now, with no personal knowledge of their God, she waited, believing quietly that these men of His would keep their word to her. She had let them down on this same thick cord, when she helped them escape the authorities that day. They would be watching for it, according to their agreement, the day Jericho would fall into their hands.

But these Israelites were different from other men, and their method of attack frayed the nerves of everyone else inside the double-walled city. It was a slow, tension-filled attack, strange and primitive and fearsome to the strong men of Jericho. The Israelites came in hordes toward the city in a silent, slow procession that struck terror within its walls. How could even the giants of Jericho defend themselves against silence and no show of military strength? Only the few men who marched at the head of the horde carried spears and arrows. The others wore long, swinging robes and carried an odd wooden object like an ark, draped in heavy curtains and resting on two poles. The others held long, curved objects in their hands, and slowly, with firm steps the long line of Israelites wound up from the encampment at Gilgal toward the high walled city, whose locked gates now seemed futile to almost every nervous citizen watching from the high walls.

The tension mounted as the strange line of conquerors came closer, close enough for Rahab to see that the curved objects were ramshorn trumpets—shophars. And after they had marched all the way around Jericho in silence, with no spear flying, and no arrow springing from a single bow, the men carrying the curved shophars placed them to their lips and split the terror-filled silence with a blast that seemed to shake the foundations of the mighty city. As silently, then, the marching Israelites turned and walked steadily back to their encampment at Gilgal. For six days the same eerie performance took place. Inside the locked city, the big men of Jericho quaked and some of them lost their senses entirely from fear.

Rahab merely waited, her family around her, the thick red cord tightly in place.

On the seventh day, the line of marching men came on again, but this time at dawn. It all looked the same. The shophar's scooping three-note wail was just as full of terror, but this time they did not turn back to Gilgal. And on a command from Joshua, their leader, their wild primitive victory shouts, deafening above the shophar blasts, started the great groan and rumble that brought down the very walls of Rahab's city!

Caleb and Salmon found her inside her house, her family around her, waiting to be rescued. One at a time they let themselves down the sturdy red rope to the ground. The promises had been kept on both sides. Rahab and her family went with the conquerors this time, out of the ruined, death-strewn city, over the crumbled walls, back to Gilgal.

Her family must have had trouble believing they were alive and safe, as they neared the Hebrew encampment that night. But not Rahab, who had believed for so long in the God whose name she did not know. We are told she married Salmon, one of the spies who visited her house, and so became a Hebrew herself, and the mother of Boaz, who married Ruth, whose son bore Jesse, the father of David, through whose line Jesus was born.

*   *   *

Two things stand out to be remembered by women today, from the story of Rahab, the harlot. First of all, God is not deterred by the darkness in a human heart. Rahab's heart was dark until she began to believe the stories she heard about the God of Abraham and Isaac. This much belief lets light into the human heart. God knows this and acts accordingly. We forget it most of the time, and in our forgetfulness, we limit the God who never gets His facts mixed up. Until there is faith in God, the human heart—every human heart is in darkness. He, God, is the Light of the world's darkness. Most of us would be apt to pass over Rahab, with a snort of condemnation, or at best, of petty disdain. After all, she was a "woman of ill repute"—a harlot. The shocking thing is not Rahab's darkness of heart *before* she believed God. The shocking thing here is that we as Christian women forget the facts about both the human heart's darkness *and* the determination of God. He did not come to condemn or show even petty disdain toward any human being. He came to save—as He saved Rahab and her family. As He saves us.

The second thing to be remembered, as I see it, is this: He does not wait for us to become perfect and in possession of only high, pure thoughts and unmixed motives before He moves through us. No human being is ever truly ready to be an instrument of God! It is the height of spiritual arrogance to think we can be. He waits only for the sign of faith that was so evident in this woman, Rahab, and then He begins to move in His redemptive power. Perhaps her motives were mixed—admittedly she wanted to save her own skin and that of her family. But her faith was there. She knew and recognized and confessed the identity and the power of the God of Israel, and He was willing to move ahead, knowing that later on, He could untangle Rahab's motives.

God, who is always in motion toward us, working with us where we are and as we are, trusts His own power to change us day by day into His own image.

9. RUTH AND NAOMI

Friends Though In-Laws

On the low, reed-covered south bank of the Arnon River, separating Moab from the land of the Israelites, three women stood weeping and clinging to one another. The two younger women, Ruth and Orpha, were Moabites; the old woman, a Jewess named Naomi, their mother-in-law. Tears came easily for all three. Ruth and Orpha were recently widowed, and their husbands were Naomi's only sons.

A long history of friction between Moab and Israel made the devotion of these three women unusual; but there they stood, weeping together, on their way back to Judah where Naomi felt they would fare better as lone women, with their men dead. Years before, Naomi, her husband and their two sons, Mahlon and Chilion, had left their home city, Bethlehem in Judah during a famine and settled in Moab. The sons married Moabite girls. Naomi's husband died first, then her sons, and now the three women stood by the river, weeping at their last sight of Moab where they had all been happy. Orpha's weeping grew helplessly, and Naomi checked her own, to comfort her daughter-in-law.

"Orpha, life must go on for us, even without them."

The young woman dropped to the ground, her sobbing uncontrollable, tears wetting her long black hair. Ruth pressed her hand to her lips to stop her own weeping and looked down at Naomi, kneeling now beside Orpha. *I must control my grief,* Ruth thought. *Dear Naomi's heart is broken too. Why should I add to her burden? It is enough that she must comfort Orpha.*

Naomi's arms were around Orpha's shoulders. "Look at me, daughter. Hold your weeping for a moment and try to think. Perhaps you should not leave Moab. You were doing fine with your grief over your husband's death. It is leaving your homeland, too, that has crushed you." The old woman pulled herself to her feet and faced both her daughters-in-law. "Go back, each of you, to your mother's home! May the Lord treat you as kindly as you have both treated me and those who have died. The Lord grant that you may find rest, each in a new husband's home."

Orpha was standing now, too, and when Naomi could say no more, she pulled them both close and kissed them.

"No, we are going back with you, Naomi, to your people."

"I beg of you, for your dear hearts' sake, go back, my daughters! Why should you go with me? Do I have any more sons within me, who could become your husbands? Go back, my daughters; go your way; I am too old to marry again. And even if I thought there was hope—if I were with a husband tonight, if I should bear sons, would you wait until they are grown up, while you are kept from having a husband?"

Orpha turned her back and wept again, but Ruth clung to Naomi.

"Orpha sees that I am right, Ruth. She sees. And she is wise."

Orpha turned suddenly and kissed her husband's mother, then ran from them, back toward her own mother's house.

"Look, Ruth, your sister-in-law has gone back to her people and to her gods; go with her!"

Ruth lifted her head from Naomi's shoulder and the sun glinted off her bright, thick hair as she spoke. "Do not urge me to desert you by turning away from you; because wherever you go, there I will go; wherever you lodge I will lodge. Your people are my people, and your God is my God. Wherever you die I will die, and there I shall be buried. Thus may God do to me and worse if anything but death separates you and me."

Naomi said no more, and the two women walked on toward Bethlehem and drew still closer together with every dusty mile of the nearly 120 which stretched between the little boundary river and Bethlehem.

*　　　*　　　*

Love is not limited by the type of relationship between two people. Love is only limited by human self-concern. We are not surprised at a deep love between two friends, between a husband and wife, between parents and their children—but a love relationship between a woman and her daughter-in-law is pathetically rare. Jokes about their hostility are the commonplace.

And yet here is a love relationhsip between a woman and her son's wife which has ridden out the centuries firmly alongside Damon and Pythias, Jonathan and David, Paul and Timothy, Jesus and His disciple, John. Was Orpha at fault for turning back to her own people? I think not. It is not a matter for blame of Orpha, rather for wonder, that Ruth's heart held such a love capacity. She was still fairly young, undoubtedly beautiful, and might easily have decided this old woman, too old to bear more sons, was no longer any responsibility of hers. Why should she ruin her entire life by saddling herself with a useless old lady? Was her poetic speech of devotion to Naomi an extension of the love she still felt for Naomi's son? Perhaps. But it also defined Ruth's heart: open, submissive, gifted with God's own capacity to love the other person. Orpha was not unusually selfish, Ruth was unusually unselfish.

More than this, Naomi's own devotion to the God of Israel had reached the heart of this girl from a pagan land. Orpha turned back to the gods of her people, Ruth moved toward the God of Abraham. There is no greater opportunity for a Christian woman to witness to her own devotion to the God she follows than in the presence of her son's wife. Now and then, but only now and then, we hear of such devotion to the Lord God. *Naomi had reached Ruth for Him.* She had lived so that He could reach through her believing heart into the darkened heart of her daughter-in-law, and now Ruth could say: "Your God is my God."

There is no better test of a woman's spiritual health than that she love her son's wife as Naomi apparently loved both Ruth and Orpha. There is no better test of a woman's spiritual vigor than the returned love of her daughter-in-law. This may take years to happen in some cases, but it can happen. Love itself is never limited by the circumstances of a relationship, because God, Himself, is never limited—except by a closed heart.

Ruth's New Faith Rewarded

When Naomi trudged back into Bethlehem with her daughter-in-law, Ruth, "the whole town was stirred because of them." Naomi had left a happy woman, with her husband, her two fine sons, their cattle and sheep. Now she was back, her men and possessions gone, and with her, a foreigner. Tongues wagged, and even her close friends had trouble recognizing Naomi, grown so old and stooped with the weight of her great grief and poverty.

"The barley season has just begun. Please let me go into the field and glean heads of grain for our food, dear Naomi," Ruth urged. "We will make a new life together here in your land. I promise I will not allow the prejudice against me to harm me. Your God is now my God."

Naomi touched Ruth's hand tenderly. "Yes, go, my daughter. Whatever has been taken from us, we must eat. God go with you."

God was guiding Ruth from the moment she walked away from Naomi that first morning to join the other women who followed the harvesters in the fields, gathering the dropped grain—the custom with women who had no other means of support. It happened that on her first day, Ruth gleaned in the fields of Boaz, a rich relative of Naomi's husband. That night she told Naomi all about him.

"You are interested in this great man, Boaz, my daughter." Naomi smiled and her old eyes which had wept for so long, twinkled a little. Ruth blushed.

"There is nothing to hang your head over, child; Boaz is one of the handsomest and kindest men in all Judah. And one of the richest."

"He was kind to me," Ruth said. "He told me I could stay right in his fields and assured me he had ordered the young men to leave me alone." She looked up. "And Naomi, Boaz also said that when I grow thirsty, I am to drink from the vessels his men set out."

The older woman chuckled. "No wonder your baskets are so full of grain. Boaz probably told the men to drop extra heads just for you!"

"He did speak to me in such a kind way."

Naomi stood up. She had an idea. "Ruth, Boaz winnows barley tonight on the threshing floor. So should I not look for a resting place for you that you may prosper? Have you not always been kind to me? Boaz is a fine man *and* a relative. See here, now! Take a bath, child, anoint yourself, dress up and tonight step down to the threshing floor!"

"But Naomi, my mother, he is such a great man!"

"Hush, daughter, and remember, don't let him see you until he is through eating and drinking. When he lies down to sleep beside his grain to protect it, watch carefully the exact spot where he lies down; then you slip in, raise the covering from his feet and lie down too."

As Naomi knew she would, Ruth obeyed her. And Boaz was even kinder than Ruth had expected, kinder and more thoughtful of her reputation. When he found her at his feet, he lit no lamp, for fear someone would see her and gossip. Boaz already loved the beautiful, quiet-mannered, devout young woman.

"He was kind, Naomi, and gracious, and he wants to marry me! But although he is a near kinsman, there is one man nearer, and before Boaz can claim me as his wife, he has to observe one Hebrew custom. It has to do with your one remaining field, Naomi."

"Ah, yes, I know," the old woman frowned and then smiled. "I know the custom, but I also know the kinsman he must see. The custom says that the nearest kinsman must buy up anything sold by a widow in order to keep it in the family. Boaz will meet this scoundrel at the city gate tomorrow in the presence of ten city elders, and offer the man the right to buy my field."

"What if the other kinsman buys it, Naomi? What then?"

"Oh, he'll snap it up, daughter, figuring he can sell it back to Boaz at a big profit. But—Boaz will surely offer you along with the field, and I know this kinsman!"

"He's prejudiced against me—like the others?"

"Happily so, yes! Mark my word, daughter, Boaz will get the field—and you."

Old Naomi was right, and Boaz was so loved and respected even by those who hated Ruth, that the people crowded around him saying, "May the Lord make the woman who will come into your house like Rachel and like Leah, who jointly built up the house of Israel."

Boaz and Ruth were married and when their child, Obed, was born, Naomi praised God, who did not, at last, leave her without a family and children to love. Even her gossiping neighbors said, "Praised be the Lord, this daughter Ruth means more to you than seven sons!"

The boy, Obed, whom Naomi cared for like her own, became the father of Jesse, whose son was David, the king.

*   *   *

It is easy to understand why the German poet, Goethe, wrote that the Book of Ruth is "the loveliest little idyll that tradition has transmitted to us." The entire story is a total victory for love. Ruth was loved eventually even by those who had despised her, because she remained so consistently lovable. The girl received love because she gave only love away.

Surely she was confused and hurt by the gossip and extreme show of prejudice against her because of her pagan ancestry, but there is no indication that she nurtured resentment or even rebellion. She went out into the fields to glean, openly, alone, facing the gossip calmly. She gave only love, so in the long run love had to come back to her. When we send our love, even if it is thrown back in our faces, it is still love when it returns!

Ruth did not rebel or defend herself against the ugly prejudice of the people of Bethlehem—she just went on loving. And at last the prejudice was overcome.

Few among us today are so adequate in the face of prejudice of any kind. I, for one, have had difficulty giving up my prejudice against those who have race prejudice! The difficulty dwindles, when we begin to love in all directions. But love cannot be legislated. It must spring from the heart of God. It must be given to us by the Holy Spirit. Paul says that: "The love of God is (already) shed abroad in our hearts."

Dare we refuse a gift we have already been given by the One who gave Himself as He did on His cross with His arms open to the whole lost, sinful world? A world which did and does include each one of us?

10. HANNAH

A Mother Who Knew How to Love

It was the vintage season, and time once more for the mild-mannered priest, Elkanah, to take his family from their home city of Ramah across the autumn-hued hills to the temple at Shiloh to worship the Lord and to bring Him offerings.

Donkeys brayed and children shouted and the servants strapped bundles securely to the little pack animals, as Elkanah and his two wives, Peninnah and Hannah, prepared to leave on the annual pilgrimage. Hannah was ready first, and as usual, she tried to be helpful with the children, none of which were her own.

"Take care, Hannah!" Peninnah's sharp voice cut through the hubbub and confusion. "It takes a *mother* to handle children. Mount your beast and leave my children to me!"

Elkanah hurried to Hannah's side, touched her hand briefly to comfort her.

It happened every year when they made the pilgrimage to Shiloh. Peninnah hated Hannah because Elkanah loved his childless wife with all his heart. Her barbs and ridicule seemed saved for what should have been a happy journey to the house of the Lord God, and every year, Hannah arrived at Shiloh, nervous and half ill from Peninnah's taunts. Knowing that Elkanah would, as usual, give Hannah a double portion on his offering day, Peninnah's jealousy and hatred built toward that day, until at feast time, Hannah was too harassed and upset to eat, and could only sit and weep.

"Hannah," her husband whispered. "Why cry and why not eat? Oh, Hannah, why are you so downhearted? Do I not mean more to you than ten sons?"

Hannah could find no words to answer this helpless, gentle husband of hers who loved her so deeply. And after everyone but Hannah had eaten and drunk his fill, as soon as she could escape unnoticed from the family group, she fled to the temple to pray.

Seated on a bench near the doorpost of the Lord's temple, old Eli, the priest, watched the weeping young woman stop a short distance away from where he sat. No sound came from her moving lips. Hannah poured out her petition silently to the Lord God from her sorrowing heart, weeping bitterly.

"O Lord of hosts, if Thou wilt actually look at Thy handmaid's trouble, wilt think of me and not forget Thy handmaid, and wilt grant Thy handmaid a son, then I will give him to the Lord all his life, and no razor shall come upon his head."

This would be an outward sign of her son's utter dedication to the Lord.

As Hannah went on praying from her heart, old Eli rose from his bench and moved close enough to watch her lips moving, to make sure his ears were not deceiving him. They were not; the sorrowing woman made no sound at all when she prayed.

"Woman!" Eli's raspy old voice shattered her concentration. "How long will you behave there as though you are drunk? Get rid of your wine!"

Hannah raised her head, her large dark eyes blurred by tears, her high-boned cheeks wet with them. "Oh, no, my master, I am a deeply grieved woman. I have drunk no wine or liquor, but I have poured out my soul before the Lord. Do not consider your maid a good-for-nothing; I have spoken all the while under stress of provocation and distress! Believe me, my lord, I am not drunk!"

Eli stared at her a moment, as though deciding about her purity and sincerity of heart. When he spoke again, his voice had gentled: "Then, go in peace, daughter, and the God of Israel will grant you what you have prayed to Him for."

A smile as deep as her sorrow came slowly to Hannah's lovely face, and after a moment or two of realization that her prayer would be answered, she sprang to her feet, rejoined the others, and ate heartily, with no hint of any more sadness.

When Elkanah went in to Hannah again upon their return to their home in Ramah, the Lord remembered her and she bore him a son, whom she named Samuel because, she said "I have asked him of the Lord."

The next autumn, when it was time to go once more to

Shiloh, Elkanah reluctantly agreed for Hannah to remain at home, since her beautiful son, Samuel, had not yet been weaned.

"When the boy is weaned, my husband, then I will take him and he will appear before the Lord and stay there for always."

"Do whatever seems best to you, Hannah. Stay home until you have weaned him, and may the Lord confirm His word."

When the time came, while the boy was still very young, Hannah took a three-year-old bullock, a bushel of flour, and a skin of wine, and brought little Samuel to the Lord's house at Shiloh. After the bullock had been slain, she took the lad to Eli and said, "Please, sir, as you live, sir, I am the woman who stood near you here in prayer before the Lord. For this little boy I prayed, and the Lord has granted me what I prayed to Him for." Hannah's voice trembled, and now the tears flowed again. Her mother-heart tore within her, but her courage held. "I have therefore handed him back to the Lord."

The small boy looked up at his mother's tears, but they did not frighten him, because her head was high.

"As long as my son Samuel lives, he is returned to the Lord."

And the small boy who had already been taught by his mother to worship God, did so that day in the house of the Lord, where he would stay for all the years of his life.

*   *   *

If Hannah had not followed through on her promise to return her son to God, we could suppose she might have prayed so fervently for a son, in order to compete with her husband's other wife, Peninnah. But Hannah kept her promise. Her motives were unmixed. She wanted a son so that he could serve the God she loved so devoutly.

It is no news to most persons that mothers are not all unselfish human beings. Many are. In fact, most persons confuse real love with possessiveness, and when things don't work out to their liking (as they never do!), they blame God or the other person because they don't receive the response they think they deserve. Just because a woman has given birth to a child in no way means she has become a saint. Much trouble between mothers and their children stems from the fact that some women seem to feel that the process of having given birth puts them in a class deserving special treatment.

In one sense it does, and their attitudes are, to me, quite understandable. Not the highest, but understandable at least. It is not a simple thing to give birth to a child, and rearing one is even more complicated. Still, most women go into it with their eyes open, and some forget that the child has nothing whatever to do with it! When a woman expects her child to prove his love by bending his life to the satisfaction of her whims, she has fallen into the trap of possessiveness, not love. Real love concerns itself, first of all, with the welfare of the loved one—never with itself.

I doubt that Hannah, had her son remained with her, would ever have uttered the familiar old mixed-motive wail: "After all I've done for you, it seems to me that you could do this or that for your poor old mother!" Hannah knew how to love, and she drew strength from her knowing.

Of course, it broke her heart to leave the little fellow forever in the temple with old Eli. But she did it, and God handled her broken heart. He had handled it before the child came, in the face of the taunts and barbs of her husband's other wife; she saw no reason why He wouldn't handle it always, under any circumstance. This kind of simple, uncomplicated, all-encompassing faith, is the most practical possession a woman can have. Hannah had it; and it was not compartmentalized in any sense. She did not have faith only to worship God in His temple; she had faith to drop her sadness and begin to *hope,* once she had poured out her heart in prayer to Him for a son. Samuel had not been born yet, but within minutes after she prayed, she dropped her sorrowing, dried her tears, let go her sadness, and ate!

She allowed God to give her the needed immunity to Peninnah's harassment, and also to her own possible doubts during the months between her prayer and the birth of her son. That Hannah was going to turn out as she did, was evident in her straightforward, unself-defensive explanation of her behavior to old Eli. After all, he jumped to a cruel conclusion about her, simply because she happened to be praying deeply from her heart, with no sound coming from her moving lips. He accused her of being drunk. What would you do in the face of an accusation like that? Would you be self-defensive? Insulted? Would you attempt to cut down your accuser? Would I? Hannah showed no sign of self-defense. She was simply truthful with Eli. She told him of her sorrow; she told him what she prayed for; she told him (with no hints of pride or wounded feelings) that she had drunk no wine or liquor. She did not act shocked at his accusation. She made no effort to put him in his place. She merely explained, with no mixed motives.

This, as I see it, was Hannah's secret. Her motives were unmixed. Her entire heart was turned toward the Lord God. And it was open.

No wonder Samuel became an authentic man of God; his mother had passed on her own uncluttered, truly believing faith to him from the day of his birth.

Faith, after all, is not measured by how we *sound* when we pray. Hannah made no audible sound at all. Faith is not measured by how noticeably we serve God. Hannah did nothing beyond bearing a child; but her faith lived and acted in God's behalf through her child, Samuel. It was of inestimable importance to the boy to have had her early training; but perhaps it was of equal importance that Hannah proved her love for her son by leaving him *free* to become his best self in the service of the Lord God.

11. ABIGAIL

A Woman With God's Own Poise

Young David had already been anointed by Hannah's son, Samuel, to be God's choice as the next king of Israel. But Saul still sat uncertainly on his throne, and because of his erratic mental condition—one day forgiving David for his imagined slights, and the next seeking to kill him—David had become a wandering shepherd. He had gathered around him six hundred followers, and although they lived off other people's property, unlike most marauding bands of nomads, David's men usually gave service in exchange for food and supplies.

Shortly after the death of old Samuel, during shearing season in the sheep and goat country west of the Dead Sea, David and his men had given unusual protection to the flocks of a rich man named Nabal, whose lavish estate was built on a high lush plateau just beyond the bare valleys and limestone hills near the city, Carmel. For days, David and his men had stood guard, forming a wall of protection around Nabal's flocks and herdsmen, as they rounded up the sheep for shearing. Their supplies were gone, and fully justified in his request, David sent ten of his men to Nabal's house to ask for food.

The large house swarmed with busy servants and guests. At shearing time, Nabal's house was always like a huge hotel, where the kitchens poured forth all manner of rich foods. David knew this, but he did not know Nabal. Because Nabal's wife, Abigail, was such a capable, intelligent woman, Nabal left the management of the feasting to her. Day in and day out, the rich man did nothing but eat and drink, so he stayed perpetually drunk. The few hours he slept each night made no difference. He awoke in the mornings for one reason only—to drink still more. Even during his rare sober moments, Nabal was a boor: rough, loud, churlish, bad-tempered.

Unfortunately, David's men met him, and not his wife, with their request for food.

"Greetings from our master, David! Peace to you! Peace to your home! Peace to all you possess!" As David's ten men made their plea for food, Nabal scowled, half-listening, swaying unsteadily on his feet, gulping his liquor from an amethyst bowl, cursing every drop he spilled. The spokesman for David finished his request, and Nabal's shepherds verified the help they had received in the hills outside Carmel. But Nabal was not impressed.

"Who is David, and who is Jesse's son?" Infuriated, he spewed a mouthful of liquor at them. "There are many servants nowadays running away from their masters! Shall I then take my food, my wine and the meat I have butchered for my own shearers, and give it to persons from I do not know where? Get out; all of you—get out!"

When David heard this, he ordered his men to gird on their swords. Two hundred remained with the supplies and four hundred, led by David himself, began their march on Nabal's estate. David's anger ran high. "So, our protecting this fellow's belongings in the desert so that he missed nothing, proved all useless; he is returning evil for good. May God do so to David's enemies and worse if, of all he has, I leave a single male alive by morning!"

The servants, anticipating David's action against them, hurried to their mistress, Abigail. As always, she listened patiently. To make amends for another bombast from her foolish husband was nothing new to Abigail, who knew him through and through. After the servants told her the facts about David's protection of their flocks, and about Nabal's vulgar behavior, they urged her to consider the whole thing carefully, warning her that David would make quick reprisal against their household.

"Consider well what you are to do, Mistress Abigail, we are sure disaster has been decided on for our master and for his entire household. We had to come to you, because our master is such a son of Belial nobody can talk to him!"

Abigail was far too wise even to try reasoning with her husband in his condition, and so she set to work on her own. In record time she oversaw the preparation and packing of enough food and wine for 600 hungry men, and mounted on an ass behind the train of animals and servants bearing the food, she followed them out into the mountainous desert where David and his men were, at that moment, coming toward her.

They met, each descending a steep mountain pass. Abigail dismounted quickly, fell on her face before David, bowed to the ground at his feet, and said, "On me, sir, falls the blame! Allow your maid, please, to address you, and listen to your servant's words."

David stared at the beautiful, refined, richly dressed woman kneeling before him. "Let my master pay no attention, I beg of you, to this worthless man, my husband, Nabal! He is just like his name—foolish, wicked, and drunk most of the time. He is a fool, but I, your maid, did not see the men my master sent. I am the only responsible one at Nabal's house—on me, sir, falls the blame for this dreadful thing."

The woman raised her face to look at David now, and he was struck with her intelligence and poise. "So then, sir," Abigail went on, "as the Lord lives and as you live, when the Lord has restrained you from bloodshed and from taking the law in your own hands, may your enemies and all who plan against you fare like Nabal!"

David's mind turned rapidly. This was surely a woman of uncommon ability and good judgment. And yet she dared to leave her home without her husband. Sensible, too, he reasoned; and his quick eyes took in the enormous load of food she had brought.

"Please pardon your maid's conduct," Abigail seemed to read his thoughts as well. "For the Lord shall certainly set you up a lasting dynasty, because you, my master, are fighting the Lord's battles, and no evil is found in you for all your life. Should anyone undertake to persecute you and to seek your life, then my master's soul will be wrapped in the bundle of life with the Lord your God."

David wondered at her words, and at the woman herself, in silence and admiration and respect.

"Then when the Lord has fulfilled all His good promises to you, my master, and has made you prince over Israel, then your heart will suffer from no self-accusation for my master's shedding blood without cause and for taking the law in his own hand. And when the Lord has prospered my master, then remember your servant girl."

David watched her rise to her feet and step modestly back a few steps. Then he said thoughtfully, as though they had been talking together for a long time, and knew each other well: "Blessed be the Lord, the God of Israel, who sent you today to meet me. Blessed be your good judgment, and blessed be you for restraining me today from the guilt of bloodshed and from taking the law into my own hands. For as surely as the Lord God of Israel lives, who kept me from hurting you, if you had not hurriedly met me, not a male around Nabal would have been left alive by the break of day."

David gratefully accepted her gifts to him and his men, and said to her from his heart, "Go back home in peace. And remember, I have listened to your voice and your words. And personally—I like you."

Abigail was too wise to tell Nabal any of this until morning. The shock was so great to him, he died soon after.

Later, David the king sent for Abigail, who became one of his eight wives.

*   *   *

Every woman with a husband who is difficult for any reason, cannot be sure that things will turn out as well as they did for Abigail. Every woman with an alcoholic husband cannot—must not be led to believe that if she obeys God, uses her highest intelligence, and acts on her knowledge of what is right, as Abigail did, she will be set free of the day-in and day-out burden of such a husband. This is not the point here.

The point, as I see it, is this: Abigail did use her highest intelligence (and in her case this was real wisdom), but she was able to do it *and* retain her poise in the process because she truly believed God. Now, here we must think through what truly believing God really means. Relevant to our story about Abigail, the woman with God's own poise, it means this: if we are to act in the tight places as though we really believe what we claim, we must realize that believing includes *seeing* realistically as God sees!

Abigail was realistic about her husband, Nabal. He was a fool, a drunkard, a crude, ridiculous man. She knew this and she *accepted* it. Her acceptance did not change him, but it did free her to avoid the pitfall of self-pity. This woman didn't have time for self-pity. She had to do her work and her husband's, too. And she did it, with the very poise of God. That she ended up as David's wife is scarcely the issue. Abigail was being Abigail *before* David came on the scene. As far as she was concerned, she would never see the handsome young man again after that day in the mountain pass. She returned home to the same old situation, and used her intelligence to wait until morning to tell her husband. That he died soon afterwards, so that she was at last free of him, is also not the point. Abigail had no idea he was going to die. She intended to go on being God's child, making the intelligent *most* of her dreadful situation before and after meeting David, and before and after Nabal's death.

Only God can give a woman poise like Abigail possessed, and God can only do it when a woman is willing to cooperate as Abigail cooperated with Him on every point.

12. RIZPAH

Only Her Suffering to Give

The first month of her strange, lonely vigil had passed, although Rizpah could not have told how long she had been there. She did not count the days, and they differed from the nights only in their intense heat and a slight change in her one occupation.

Rizpah, the once beautiful concubine of Saul, now an old woman, had one change of occupation on her lonely rock from day to night. At night she kept a fire burning against the chill wind, and a lighted torch ready when a wild animal prowled close by, drawn by the stench of the decaying bodies of the seven dead men she guarded. Two of them were her own beloved sons by King Saul, whom she had loved with all her passionate woman heart. The other five were the dead bodies of Saul's grandsons, all killed in an attempt to placate God for an old, half-forgotten sin of Saul against the people of Gibeon. By night, Rizpah drove away wild animals; by day, big voracious scavenger birds, which swooped and wheeled about the blackening, broken bodies over which she watched.

The grieving woman had no power to prevent the murders of her sons, but there was no one to stop her from watching over their poor bodies. And she believed God that one day, when the rains came at last, the dear dishonored bodies would be noticed and buried.

A famine gripped the land, and King David had ordered the killings to appease God, according to his belief that sin brought famine and flood. Saul had filled Rizpah's life, and his two sons had been her only solace—her only reason for living, after Saul was dead. Now, there remained only one reason for living through her strange days and nights alone on the wide, flat rock above the City of David—to protect her two boys' bodies from animals and vultures until they could have a decent burial. Nothing would be done, she knew, until the rains came and the

famine ended. Then, perhaps David would believe it good
to bury these seven dead men, forgotten by everyone but
Rizpah, and the few who scorned or cheered her lonely
vigil from a distance.

Two months passed. Three. Four. Now, the stench was
not so bad; the seven broken forms still hanging from their
gallows swung more lightly in the quick afternoon wind,
and in the chill night gusts off the higher portion of the
mountain. They were almost skeletons now, but Rizpah
had protected them—Saul's five grandsons as well as her
own sons. She had hung them with sackcloth and had
wrapped herself in it, too, and hour after hour she sat huddled under it for shade from the sun, or shivered in it at
night, as the seven bodies swung in the wind and kept the
shadows changing, weird and skeletal on the bare rock,
when the moon shone brightly in the heavens.

Rizpah kept her watch, and slept as little as possible,
forcing consciousness by reliving the luxurious, happy,
love-filled years when she had been one of Saul's favorite
concubines. She even stopped weeping sometimes when she
remembered one particularly beautiful gown she had worn
at his court. Once she almost smiled at what he had said to
her. But Rizpah's days and nights were mainly welded
together by sorrow and tears. As her weariness grew, her
grief grew with it. She did not once grow accustomed to
the loss of all that she had loved; she only grew accustomed to springing to her feet to protect the dear,
shriveled bodies against any harm.

She had loved Saul. Then Saul was killed. She had loved
his sons, and now they were only grotesque, silent remind-
ers that sorrow would fill her life forever.

At last, when the rains came, someone reminded David
of the seven corpses and of Rizpah. He had them buried
with the bones of Saul and Jonathan in a family grave.

Rizpah could stop watching, and wait now, with her sorrow, until she, too, could die.

*   *   *

Under somewhat different circumstances, women still
watch and wait, with only their sorrow for companionship.
Their sorrow and God. Rizpah had Him, too, otherwise
she might have lost her mind through those lonely five
months on her rock guarding the seven dishonored corpses
with her frail body.

What is the answer for the human heart drenched in grief and sorrow? What do we say to those whose lives have been stripped by death (or worse) of every joyful thing? Is there an answer? Not a pat one, surely. But there is a way of making use of grief and sorrow, because God *exists*.

As I have written this book, the newspapers carried the tragic story of a young mother whose entire family—her husband and all of her children but one, were killed in an automobile accident. What can this woman do? How can she learn to live with her grief?

Because Jesus Christ has come, she has access to more than poor Rizpah, who lived and grieved in the semi-twilight years before His coming. But Rizpah or a woman now, will both be haunted by one unanswerable question: why did it happen? In Rizpah's case, sorrow came, humanly speaking, because of the sins of Saul, the man she loved. Yet Rizpah bore the sting of it. Did she sit there on her rock and struggle to understand? Or did God break through to her in His reality—as He has now broken through to us in Jesus Christ?

We now know that all tragedy is *not* the direct result of someone's conscious sin. The woman whose husband and children were killed in the automobile accident had done no conscious wrong. True, she was driving the family car which left the road when she fell asleep at the wheel. But she had been up all night before their planned vacation trip doing the hundred and one things only a mother can do to get her family ready. She was being a good mother—not wise to try to drive with no sleep, but her intentions were not sinful ones. This is obvious to anyone. I have prayed often that someone could help her see that to blame herself would be foolish. Still, the question haunts the human heart when tragedy strikes—Why?

God anticipated our question. On His cross Jesus cried: "My God, *why* hast Thou forsaken Me?" He has even cried "Why?" for us. And in the process He has laid down His life so that we would be enabled by His Spirit within us to cooperate with Him in making creative *use* of our sorrow and grief. Our God is a Redeemer God. He wastes nothing.

There are still Rizpahs in our world. Perhaps you are one. Perhaps you know one. God is reminding us all in Jesus Christ that where He is, there can be no such thing as a total blackout of joy forever. In the semi-twilight of her time, Rizpah did what we must do. She *gave*. All she knew how to give, she gave there on her lonely rock, to Saul's memory and to her sons. *Giving* unlocks our own hearts to God's comfort and His new plans for our lives after tragedy and grief have done their worst.

Our God is a Redeemer God. He wants to waste nothing! Not even our tears.

13. ESTHER

A Woman of Courage

In the year 482 B.C., during the Babylonian captivity of the Jews, a young and beautiful Jewess named Esther stood talking excitedly with her cousin Mordecai, who had given her a home after the death of her mother and father.

"This is a golden opportunity for you, Esther. The king has disposed of his queen, Vashti, for refusing to be put on display along with his other royal possessions, and now all the beautiful virgins are being called together to be presented to him. From these assembled maidens Xerxes (Ahasuerus) will choose a new queen. You can be that queen, Esther!"

"I will obey you, my cousin, as I have always done—but I admire Queen Vashti for remaining a queen in her show of courage. The idea of the king's asking her to do such a thing!" Esther's dark eyes flashed scornfully, and as always her spirit delighted her cousin, Mordecai, an official at the palace gate.

Esther took her place among all the lovely young girls presented by their families at the palace to Hege, the eunuch in charge of the king's women. During the entire year in which the young applicants were beautified with myrrh and balms and perfumes before being presented before the king, Esther grew in favor with Hege, whom she obeyed willingly as she always obeyed her cousin, Mordecai. Not a day passed that Mordecai, anxious for her progress, didn't check on her, warning her to keep her Jewish blood a secret.

When at last the evening came when Esther was led before the king to spend her night alone with him, she was flushed and more beautiful than ever with excitement. The splendor of the pagan court stretched before the devout Jewish girl in a dancing blur of black and white marble, alabaster, linen and purple draperies caught with silver rings, gold and silver couches—even the floor on which she stood before the king was paved with mother-of-pearl.

The generous, amoral, pleasure-loving Xerxes was accustomed to the magnificence of his palace, but he had
never seen beauty like Esther's. Hege had carefully draped
her in flowing robes of gold and purple; with his own
hands, he had set her black hair with jewels, and her dark
olive skin shone beneath the ointments and pagan cos-
metics. Her large eyes caught the king's and held them.

From all the numbers of beautiful young women, Xerxes chose Esther, the orphaned Jewess, to be his queen,
who, unknown to him, worshiped the Lord God of Israel.

Everyone who knew her loved her, and in no time, with
the confidence of the palace officials and servants, she
soon discovered that her people, the Jews, had a dangerous
enemy in her husband's favorite official, Haman. Haman
was brilliant, ruthless, desperately ambitious—an ancient
Hitlerian type who would stop at nothing to promote himself. When he learned of Haman's new decree that all Jews
must bow at his appearing, Esther's cousin, Mordecai,
refusing to bow to anyone but the Lord God, became
Haman's most hated enemy.

Using his influence with the king, who cared more for
pleasure than for his duties as ruler of Persia, Haman
manipulated a royal decree that all Jews—men, women
and children—would be killed. Mordecai went at once to
Queen Esther, urging her to appear before the king herself
and plead for her people.

"He hasn't called for me to come in to him for 30 days,
my cousin. And you know that anyone who enters his
court without being called is executed at once! Unless he
extends his golden sceptor to the intruder—there is but one
penalty—death."

"Do you not think I know what I am asking you to do,
Esther, my queen, my beloved cousin, whom I love as my
own child? Do you not think I know it could mean your
very life? But if you do not help us, it can mean the lives
of every member of our race in Persia! And who knows
but you have come to the kingdom for such a time as
this?"

Queen Esther faced her cousin for a long, silent moment.
"Go and gather all the Jews who are available and fast for
me; do not eat or drink for three days, night and day. I,
too, and my maids will similarly fast. Then, in spite of the
injunction that no one enters without being called, I will go
to the king." She lifted her head almost imperceptibly.
"And if I perish, I perish."

*   *   *

The name of the Lord God is not mentioned once in the entire book of Esther, but He is seen in constant action in almost every fast-moving development in this story of the God-fearing queen of the pagan king of Persia.

We must keep in mind that these ancients were primitive people, by our standards, now that Christ has come. Much of their behavior, we could question. Even Mordecai's urging Esther to keep her Jewish blood a secret, so that she might trick the king into choosing her, could be called less than God's best. But, as He has always done, God was working in the main stream of human history, using as much of human nature as possible in order to keep His plan moving. These Israelites, scattered into a pagan land from their Holy City of Jerusalem by Nebuchadnezzar, had to be protected. With this in mind, undoubtedly, Esther was sent into Xerxes' kingdom, as Mordecai said, "for a time like this." From the remnant of this once powerful Hebrew nation, God's Son would come. Jehovah worked to preserve this remnant through any human means at hand. Despite their lack of understanding of certain of His higher ways, He knew Mordecai and Esther to be devout believers in the Most High. And so, He chose this woman, Esther, to use her influence with a pagan king who did not believe in Him.

God worked with and through Esther as only He knew her to be. To her inherent courage, He added His own, and Esther's good mind was made up. "I will go to the king; and if I perish, I perish."

Women then and today are being called upon by the Lord God to show this kind of courage. Not in such glamorous surroundings or in such exciting circumstances; but called upon by God to show their maximum courage. And now, as then, He is always willing to add to our inherent courage, His own.

Also a Woman of Cunning

Three days after her meeting with Mordecai, Queen Esther, dressed in royal purple, her head banded in gold, walked uninvited into the inner court facing the royal hall where her husband, the king, sat on his high, ornate throne.

He looked up annoyed, then his bearded face softened, and he reached at once for his golden scepter. How had he been foolishly occupied with other matters and so neglected his beautiful queen for so long? Holding the scepter still outstretched, as Esther walked close enough to touch its golden tip, the king spoke to her intently: "What is on your mind, Queen Esther? What is your wish? It will be granted you if it were half the kingdom." The sensuous king reached toward her now, smiling.

Esther moved no closer, but replied beguilingly, "If it please your majesty, let the king and Haman attend the banquet I have prepared for the king."

"Get Haman at once!" ordered Xerxes, relieved and delighted that her request was so pleasant. "Get Haman at once, so that we may both comply with Esther's wish."

As Xerxes and Haman were drinking their wine at Esther's banquet, the king grew mellow and attentive. "Now, my queen, tell me, what is your wish? You must have more on your mind than a mere banquet. What is your petition? Even if it is half my kingdom, it will be granted you!"

Esther smiled at him. Her only request, she declared, was that he and Haman would attend still a second banquet the next day.

Haman went home that night, swollen with pride, convinced he was making great headway, not only with the king, but with his queen as well. His wife and his friends bolstered his ego with more praise, but suddenly Haman's face darkened.

"Yet all this remains unsatisfactory to me, so long as I see Mordecai the Jew seated in the royal gate!"

"Then stop being so backward, my husband," his wife, Zaresh, said sharply. "Have a gallows erected eighty feet high, and tell the king the first thing in the morning that Mordecai should be hanged on it!" The woman laughed. "Then you can happily accompany the king to the queen's banquet—with nothing to mar your pleasure."

The idea appealed to Haman, and he ordered a gallows constructed at once.

God's hand is seen at work once more that night. Xerxes, the king, could not sleep, and he ordered his record book of memorable events brought out so that he could read away the hours. In it he found the detailed account of an almost forgotten event which happened soon after Esther became his queen. Since she was so much in his thoughts that night, he had read it carefully and remembered well that Mordecai, through a message sent to the king by Esther, had saved his life when two of his doorkeeping eunuchs had planned to assassinate him.

"What honor of distinction has been given Mordecai for this deed?" The courtiers sitting up in attendance on the sleepless king replied, "Not a thing has been done for him."

A sudden confusion in the outer court caught the king's attention. "Who's there?" he called. It was Haman, unable to wait until morning, come to suggest the execution of Mordecai on the already erected gallows.

Xerxes looked quizzically at Haman, now plainly suspicious of him. "Haman," the king asked, "what should be done for a man the king is glad to honor for a great deed?"

The king's suspicion of him was evident to everyone but Haman, himself, so blinded was he by hate and greed.

With flourishes and dramatic gestures, Haman pranced before the king, describing just the kind of royal honor he felt was surely about to be his own. He would robe the man with one of the king's own cloaks, set him on one of the king's own horses, and have him ride in pomp through the city square.

The king jumped to his feet and shouted, "Hurry, then! Get that robe and that horse, Haman, and do so to Mordecai, the Jew who sits at the royal gate! And Haman—let nothing be omitted of all you have suggested."

Instead of the comfort of watching Mordecai's execution, Haman was forced to carry out the king's command himself to honor Mordecai, and then to go in shame and fury to Esther's banquet. When the men were once more drinking their wine, the king again asked Esther's pleasure. Once more, he offered her half his kingdom.

But Esther answered, "If it pleases your majesty, then may my life be granted me at my petition, and my people at my request."

"Your people, Esther? Your life?"

"We have been sold, I and my people," Esther went on steadily, admitting her Jewish blood to him for the first time, "sold to be destroyed, to be killed, to be obliterated. I beg you for our lives, my king, my husband!"

The king stood up, "Who is the man who dared contemplate such a thing?"

"An oppressor, sire, an enemy—this wicked Haman!"

Haman cowered in terror at the king's fury. And in wild, foolish desperation, when the king strode into the garden to quiet his rage, Haman attempted to seduce Esther, pleading for his life which now lay in the hands of this Jewish woman. The king caught him in his act of boldness with Esther, and what Haman hoped might save his life, brought it to an immediate end.

He was hung at once on the gallows he had caused to be built for Mordecai.

Esther had been sent for just this time, and although His name is not mentioned in the Biblical account, God had been with her to honor her courage and her cunning.

*   *   *

Esther was not only a woman of courage, she was a woman of great cunning. Her first appearance before the king was a risky one—here, she had need only of her courage. But after she found favor with him, she put her excellent mind to work. She did not plunge in begging for the lives of her people that day, but set up two banquets with Haman, her enemy, as her guest. She flattered Haman, knowing he would trip himself in his zeal to persecute her cousin. He did—all the way.

She did not fall into the trap tumbled into by so many women when they allow their emotions to rule the movement. Esther used her head, even though her heart was heavy with fear for her own life as a Jewess, and for the lives of her people.

Jesus said we were to be as gentle as doves, but as wise as serpents. Esther was both. The combination worked. We are told in James' letter that when we are in need of wisdom beyond our own, God will supply it. I like the fact that James bothered to add that God would not belittle us for asking. Why should He? God knows more clearly than we know that we are all faced with situations that require wisdom beyond our innate intelligence. God supplied Esther with His wisdom in the tight places, just as He is eager to supply us in our times of need.

He cannot do this, however, if we are plunging ahead, blinded, as was Haman, propelled by our wild-winging emotions. Any woman who knows God, has access to His wisdom at any time, under any circumstances; her part is to keep her emotions under control, and her mind open to His wisdom, which He is always eager to give.

14. JOB'S WIFE

No Communication With Her Husband

Job and his wife had lost everything but each other. Bandits had killed their servants and stolen every pack animal. Their herds and flocks had been struck by lightning. Now they lay blackened and stiff across the once fertile fields. Job, himself, was covered with boils and forced to sit day after day in the stench of the refuse heap outside the city when still another loathesome disease (probably leprosy) struck his once healthy body. He and his wife had seen their children crushed to death when a fierce wind collapsed the house in which they lived.

Total tragedy ripped its way across both their lives —God seemed dead.

And yet, neither Job nor his wife thought God dead. When Job watched one tragedy follow another, this righteous man, who felt God prospered him because of his righteousness, rent his robe, shaved his head, fell upon the ground and worshiped, saying: "Naked I came forth from my mother's womb, and naked I shall return; the Lord gave and the Lord has taken away; blessed be the name of the Lord."

But when Job was afflicted with the dread disease, and sat in the ashes scraping his sores and moaning in physical as well as mental anguish, his wife approached him crying: "Look at you, Job! Do you still hold fast to your integrity? Bid God farewell, and die!"

Neither believed God dead. But both saw Him with totally different eyes.

"You talk as one of the foolish women would talk, wife," Job admonished her in his suffering. "Are we to receive only what is good from God and are we to receive no misfortune?"

Surely Job was far from understanding the seemingly unexplained and undeserved suffering through which he and his wife were passing. It is well known that none of his friends who visited him understood either. They did what so many well-intentioned people still do—blamed it on some sin of Job's or some deviation from the doctrine they all clutched earnestly. Their long-winded arguments fell flat on Job's ears. Life, as he was living through it now, simply did not fit into the pat framework of their doctrinal emphasis. And yet Job knew God was somehow in charge.

Here we see one of the brightest, most highly illuminated instances when all men living before Christ were forced to trust God blindly, with scarcely a shred of understanding. The most Job could have been expected to do, he did. He kept on believing God would somehow triumph, even though, in the semi-darkness of life before Jesus Christ, he could only believe that "God taketh away"; that man received misfortune also from God.

In retrospect, those of us whose insights are lighted by the fact of Christ, know that "every good gift cometh down from the Father of lights, in whom there is no shadow of turning." Surely we can no more blame God for the death of a loved one, or a terrible automobile accident, than we can blame Him for the death of Jesus!

We now know that although sin and suffering are somehow still in the world, God does not will them or send them. Rather, He permits them and *then* makes creative use of them if we are willing. Job could not have known this, but after he had ultimately repented for his self-righteousness, he acted in a way which God could honor as surely as if he had known. God *only* asks that we trust Him, making use of all the light we have, and then go on trusting Him in our remaining darkness. This Job did.

To trust God when your friends condemn you, your fellow townspeople shun you, when even the last remaining loved one merely nags you and adds salt to your wounds by turning away from you in your misery because your breath is obnoxious—this is faith in action. Job had this kind of faith in God. His wife, after slinging her sarcastic dart: "Do you still hold fast to your integrity?," not only urged that Job forget God, curse Him, and die, she ultimately could stand the sight nor the smell of her diseased, suffering husband no longer, and turned away.

Through all his agony, Job did not remain pious and submissive; he was too confused, too torn by tragedy, too much in pain. But he did continue to *think* as clearly as his knowledge of God would allow. And ultimately, by means

of his suffering, he came to see his own need for repentance. In a small, dim way, God broke through with the
fact that his prosperity had not been a cheap, superficial
reward from God for "being good." Job, at last, seemingly
began to see that God intends good to all mankind; a small
shaft of the same light that fell from the cross of Christ
broke through. When Job saw that it was not his own piety
that brought his great prosperity, he repented of his pride
in that piety, and God quieted his heart and eased his suffering. Later, back with the same shallow, superficial
woman who was his wife, he once more had children—even grandchildren: ". . . the Lord blessed the latter
days of Job more than the earlier."

In spite of his intense suffering, Job *thought through* to
his own need for repentance. Then he could raise his eyes
to heaven and cry: "I know that Thou canst do all things,
and that no plans of Thine can be foiled . . . I then have
expressed what I did not understand, things too wonderful
for me . . . Shall I question Thee any more? Thou hast in-
formed me. Heretofore I had heard *of* Thee by the hearing
of the ear, but now my eye sees Thee: wherefore, I retract
and repent in dust and ashes."

Job began at that point to *know* that His Redeemer
lived. He could now associate the "high and lifted up" God
of his past religious tradition, with the *living* God who
enabled him to *see through* to reality for himself, even
though he could not fully understand. He no longer saw
God as merely a reward-giving Father, spoiling certain
members of the human race who followed a certain set of
rules. He began to see God as the Redeemer, who held
within His being the power to change men, as well as to
make creative use of the unexplained suffering which came
to them.

*   *   *

Whether Job's wife ever came to see as her husband saw,
we do not know. The only account we have of her indicates strongly to me that she typified the kind of woman
who had no real communication with her husband. She
bore his children and was no doubt a dutiful wife. Perhaps
to the limits of her capacity, she loved Job. Her caustic
remark: "Bid God farewell, and die!" has been interpreted
as indicating her heart was so torn at seeing him suffer, she

could bear it no longer; better to see him quiet and painless in death. Those of us who have watched loved ones suffer intense physical pain can understand this.

But in the breath before that remark, she had done an act of out-and-out nagging: "Do you still hold fast to your integrity?" Job felt his suffering was undeserved because of his devout life, and he continued to uphold his own integrity. At that point, God had not gotten through to him with the necessity for all men to repent before God. And this woman hit him when he was thoroughly down, at his tenderest spot, saying in effect: "Do you still feel so upright now that all this has happened to you?"

Such total misunderstanding of her deep thinking husband's personality leads me to one conclusion: they had never really had communication with each other. This was one wife who really did not understand her husband! Nor did she make any effort to follow his profound attempts to understand his plight. She threw up her hands quickly, swamped by the seemingly unending tragedy around them, and urged him to do the same.

She saw her husband strictly from her own viewpoint, not at all from his. We all have a touch of Job's wife in us today. And with far less excuse for it than she had! God has come to us in the Person of Jesus Christ, giving not only the best demonstration of what it means to *identify* with another person, but bringing with Him through His Holy Spirit, the power to do it.

Jesus came down to earth and identified with us entirely. He got into it with us. We have no reason whatever to doubt that He knows what it's like to *be* us. He "emptied Himself" of any self-concern whatever and began to live out His Holy Life in our midst, from *our* side.

Job's wife lived long, long before this greatest Event in human history. We live *after* it, and are empowered from within to be able to "get into it" with our loved ones. Tensions ease all around in any heartbreaking situation, when just one person is showing true, objective understanding of another. Women are usually the key personalities in most human tangles, and much of the confusion around us would ease at once, if only a few women would begin steadily to *identify* with the other person.

Until there is true identification, there can be no workable communication between any two persons, even when they live in prosperity and success, surrounded by their families, as did Job and his wife. When tragedy struck, it was only made clear that there had never been any true communication between this good man and his wife.

If you can only give orders to the other person when a difficult situation arises, pray—pray for the gift of true communication.

15. MARY, MOTHER OF JESUS

A Young Woman Chosen by God

A round faced, olive-skinned Hebrew girl in her late teens sat grinding barley with a mortar and pestle in the front yard of her father's house in Nazareth, a backward little hill town in northern Galilee. Her name was Mary, and next to the Lord God, she loved her father's gentle neighbor, Joseph, whose carpentry shop was near their home. It was spring, and Mary sang as she ground the barley grains; small red and brown birds in the trees above her sang, too. She had just become engaged to marry Joseph, the tall, bearded, kindly man whose strong hands shaped such smooth ox yokes and cradles and well buckets from the hard woods in the hills around Nazareth.

The song she sang was a Psalm of joy and praise to the God of her fathers. Mary's young life had known no touch of sorrow or pain, only joy, and now her cup ran over with it. A redstart sang a sudden solo on a low limb right above her head, and she stopped grinding and laughed aloud with the bird.

And then her laughter stopped abruptly. Someone else was there with her in the yard under the trees! She still held the stone pestle in one smooth, brown hand, as she stared into the face of the kindest and most beautiful Being she had ever seen. His voice was clear and quiet.

"Greeting, favored lady! The Lord is with you."

Sensing her fear, the Visitor went on talking even more gently. "Have no fear, Mary, for you have found favor with God. And observe, you will conceive in your womb and give birth to a Son and you shall call Him Jesus. He shall be great and shall be called the Son of the Highest, and the Lord God shall give Him the throne of His father

David. He shall be King over the house of Jacob forever; there shall be no end to His kingdom."

The young girl was sitting bolt upright on her short-legged grinding stool, her dark gray eyes wide with wonder and perplexity and confusion, but her fear was gone. After a long moment, she caught her breath enough to ask: "But—how shall this be, since I have no husband yet?"

"The Holy Spirit shall come upon you, Mary, and the power of the Highest shall overshadow you and therefore that holy Offspring shall be called—God's Son."

Mary dropped the pestle unnoticed and covered her face with her hands. The message was more than she could bear. As though to help her cope with the wonder, the bright Visitor stepped a little closer to where she sat and began to tell her about someone she knew well, someone close to her and familiar.

"Your cousin Elizabeth is to be mother of a son in her old age, Mary. This is her sixth month, who was called sterile!"

The girl raised her eyes again. "Elizabeth?"

"Nothing is impossible with God," the Angel said.

She had never heard God's voice with her ears before, but her heart recognized Him well. Relieved and awed by the familiar recognition, she bowed before the Angel and said the only thing Mary's simple, committed, open heart could have said at that moment: "Here I am, the Lord's servant girl. Let it be with me as you say."

And then the heavenly Visitor was gone.

*   *   *

Every devout Hebrew woman among the remnant of those still faithful to the Lord God hoped and prayed that the promised Messiah would come through her. Everyone, perhaps, but the humble, young Hebrew girl, Mary. I somehow doubt that Mary had even thought of praying that she might be the mother of the promised Redeemer of Israel. If she did, surely she prayed with totally unmixed motives. God had found her heart and her motives utterly clear and directed toward Him only.

Otherwise He could not have chosen her.

This moment in which Mary was visited by the Angel Gabriel is full of meaning for us—the reward of consecration, devotion, purity of life. She had "found favor with God." These meanings have been noted through all the years since the gospel account of the birth of Jesus was written.

And they are worth endless meditation on the part of today's woman. But for now, consider this not so recognized meaning: after she recovered somewhat from her first shock at actually *seeing* and *hearing* the Messenger from heaven, Mary's composure returned. As soon as her physical shock lessened, she felt quiet, at home. For all her 17 or 18 years on earth, she had held close, consistent, intimate conversation with the Lord God. She had never seen a heavenly being, nor heard a heavenly voice with her ears, but her heart had heard Him speak, and when her heart took over, she was poised and definite.

Quite naturally she asked how this could be since she had never known a man. But as soon as the Angel explained that the Spirit of the God whom she knew so well would overshadow her, her fear vanished, and she was quiet inside. Her awe must have increased—actually, there hadn't been time for her to think very far, but she didn't need to analyze after that moment of familiar recognition. If the Lord God was going to bring it about, she could relax and rest, knowing that whatever He did, would be good and right. Mary knew this because she *knew* God Himself. Surely she was filled with awe and wonder, but now she knew there would be no stranger involved. It would be her Lord, Himself, and her reply came naturally and quietly.

"Here I am. Let it be with me as you say."

This required no agony of decision on Mary's part—no moment of deep struggle to decide whether she was going to obey this heavenly command. She was already committed to this God who would send His Son through her; there was no need to recommit herself, that was a settled fact, long before Gabriel came to her under the trees in her father's yard.

She needed only a moment to ask a human question, to recognize the familiar voice of God, and her answer came freely, wholeheartedly.

When God speaks to us, requesting obedience, what happens? Do we need only a momentary adjustment? Do we need only to ask one or two natural questions as Mary asked? Or do we have to go through the whole thing again? Do we have to struggle in order to decide whether or not we will obey Him?

Those of us whose commitments to God are on the

installment plan, just don't get asked by Him to do the vital things. He knows us just as He knew Mary. Our God is not the kind of God whose "favor" has to be curried. Any woman can be called by God, any woman can find favor with God, if her heart is committed once and for all, as Mary's heart was committed to the Lord God.

When God calls, we need *only* to be sure it is His voice, and obedience is automatic, *if* we have spent time with Him as Mary had, and *if* we are in the daily round (even when He isn't asking something big of us) truly His "servant girls."

God Included Joseph

The secret young Mary carried shut her away at first from her family—even from Joseph. How could she tell them? Would anyone believe her? She moved through the days in her father's house, obedient as always to her parents, taking her full share of responsibility, but strangely alone, full of joy and wonder, closed in with the Lord God Himself, behind a high wall of exhilaration and promise.

She would have to tell them eventually, but shortly after her visit from the Angel, Mary made preparations for a trip to her cousin Elizabeth's home in the hill country near Jerusalem. Old Elizabeth would be the one human being with whom she could talk freely. The Angel had said that she, too, would give birth to a child—another kind of miracle, but a miracle just the same at Elizabeth's advanced age. The two women could talk together and some of the high wall of aloneness would come down. Mary would then be able to tell Joseph and her parents. The young girl did not need to see Elizabeth in order to have her faith verified. She knew God's Son was going to be born through her pure young body. She had God's own word for that. But her three months spent with Elizabeth did help give her balance. When she returned to Nazareth, she told them quietly, and they all saw a wisdom about her and a strength they had not seen before.

Even Joseph, faced with the prospect of his beloved Mary giving birth to a child conceived before their marriage, was kind. He offered to give her a letter of divorcement and keep it quiet. But Joseph was frightened because the Hebrew law called for death by stoning for an unmarried woman with child. His heart was torn in many directions, but he did not believe that Mary had lied to him. Joseph knew she would be the mother of the promised Messiah, but God gave Joseph further assurance.

"I believed you, Mary," the big, soft-spoken man said to her excitedly a few days after she returned from Hebron. "I believed you when you told me, but God bothered to reassure me in a dream last night."

"Did the Angel of the Lord appear to you, too, Joseph?"

"Yes, Mary, and he said, 'Joseph, son of David, be not afraid to marry Mary, for what is conceived in her is from the Holy Spirit. She will give birth to a son and you will call Him Jesus, for He will save His people from their sins.' When I awoke, I remembered the words of our prophet, Isaiah; 'The virgin shall be with child and shall bear a son and they shall name him Immanuel, which means, God with us.' I knew that prophecy was about you, Mary."

And their faith was increased as they watched the Lord God do all that was needed to give simple folk like them the certainty they had to have. They understood little, but they knew the Lord Himself was acting.

Mary and Joseph were married as they had planned before the Angel came.

*　　*　　*

God did not exclude Joseph. Not only did He send the Angel to him in a dream to verify what Mary had told him, but He made Joseph a human part of the divine plan, too.

"She will give birth to a son and *you* will call Him Jesus, for He will save His people from their sins."

According to custom, Joseph would name the Baby. When God acts, He never shuts people out. This is not His way. And even though He told Joseph that the Baby would be born of the Holy Spirit, He gave Joseph full responsibility as the Child's earthly father. I can't help believing that Joseph was part of the reason God was free to choose Mary. He knew they were in love with each other and planned to spend their earthly lives together. He wanted His Son to grow up in a normal, devout home, influenced and trained by God-fearing parents. Jesus was conceived by the Holy Spirit, but God Himself gave Joseph the responsibility of being His earthly father.

This entire story backs up the premise that God never overpowers us with His might or His plans. Always, He moves according to what He knows we can take, right in the stream of human history. He did not ask Mary to do an eccentric thing. He asked her to do a terrible and glorious thing, but in all its eternal enormity and greatness, God did all He could do to make it bearable for Mary and Joseph. This was to be an act of God directly, but then the good daily routine of family life would take over. Jesus was to have an earthly father. God honored Joseph, by selecting him to be the head of the house where Jesus would grow up.

The Holy Spirit of God Himself, overshadowed Mary, but in every other way, Joseph was included in the divine plan.

Mary's Son Is Born

The Holy Spirit had overshadowed Mary in the early spring, and toward the end of that year, in December, when it was almost time for the Child to be born, Joseph told Mary the disturbing news.

"Caesar Augustus had decreed that all the world should be taxed, Mary, and this means a complete census must be taken. Since we are of the line of David, we will have to make the journey to Bethlehem where we were both born."

"Why are you frowning, Joseph? If we have to go, we will go."

"But you, Mary—it's almost time for the Baby to be born!"

Mary's voice remained quiet and steady. "God knew about the census, Joseph. I'm sure He knew before Caesar knew he was going to demand it. God also knew when the Baby would be born. We have nothing to fear."

Joseph walked the seventy miles beside the small donkey on which Mary rode from Nazareth to Bethlehem, caring as best he could for her every need. He found the most comfortable places possible for frequent rest for her, and when night overtook them between the small cities en route, often he would cradle her in his arms as she slept, forcing himself to stay awake to keep off wild animals and the chill night dampness.

The people streamed toward Bethlehem from all directions, and since most of them could travel faster than Joseph and Mary, the inns were all filled up when they arrived the night Mary's Baby was about to be born. Leaving Mary with an older woman they met on the way, Joseph

ran frantically all over Bethlehem, begging for a bed for
her when she gave birth to her Child. He found none, but
when the Baby came, Mary was on a clean pile of straw, as
comfortable as Joseph could make her, in a stable warmed
against the night chill by the bodies of the animals who
alone but for faithful Joseph, witnessed the coming of the
Saviour of the world.

The sleepy cattle lowed and the sleepy sheep bleated
Him welcome, and His mother wrapped Him tenderly and
carefully in the swaddling clothes she had brought along
from Nazareth. There was no other welcome for Him in
the crowded city of Bethlehem, but out on the hills a small
band of shepherds, keeping watch over their flocks through
the chill night, had seen and heard His heavenly welcome.
As the Baby was being born, an Angel of the Lord appeared to them out there in their field, and the glory of the
Lord shone all around them. To quiet their fears, the
Angel had told them not to be afraid, that there was good
news of great joy for all the people of the known world.

Guided by the message of this heavenly Visitor, these
simple shepherds found Him with Mary and Joseph in the
stable dug into the hillside behind one of the big inns in
Bethlehem and worshiped Him.

After eight days, according to Hebrew law, Mary and
Joseph had the baby circumcised and named Him Jesus,
both of them knowing and believing that somehow He
would save His people from their sins.

Twelve hundred miles away in a distant, strange land,
some astronomers saw a new star that night, and set out at
once to find Him. The people of Bethlehem, and the hun-
dreds of rioting, laughing, cursing visitors, were unaware
of what had taken place in the hillside stable, but men were
looking for a Saviour in far off places, too, and so these
men began the long trip toward Bethlehem in Judea.

Mary held her Baby in her arms and pondered in her
heart so much more than she could speak about, even to
Joseph.

*   *   *

Every woman who has ever borne a child can only try to
imagine what Mary must have felt the night He came. She
was not an educated woman, nor wise with years. She was
little more than a child herself, but her life had been clear
enough and her commitment to God so all inclusive, that

He could make His entrance into human history through her.

It is not surprising that we are never given any of Mary's actual words after she pondered these things in her heart. We are told that she kept them there. What else could she have done? Even if she had been educated, could her thoughts have been expressed? Birth itself is strange and holy enough. To have given birth to Life Himself, locked her lips.

Every Hebrew woman prayed to be the mother of the Messiah, but God chose Mary, knowing that pride in this service to Him would never strain her thoughts. He could trust Mary with her thoughts. It is rather easy to *appear* to be humble. Most of us can calculate far enough in advance to manage outward humility in a certain set of circumstances. But true humility, of the kind Mary possessed, can only be given by God to a totally single-minded person. Mary was willing to go through with the strange Birth—pregnant before the legal year of her engagement was up—only because she loved God with all her heart. Only because her motives were totally unmixed. Now that the Child had come, she could be trusted with her thoughts. They were holy thoughts, glorifying God, stimulating only wonder and awe and reverence in everyone who contacted her and her Child.

God had entered the mainstream of human history in person, in the Person of Mary's Baby, Jesus, and with Him came, not only hope for the world, but responsibility and obligation to God which this simple Jewish girl could only ponder silently in her own heart.

A Sword Through Mary's Soul

After the 33 days set aside by law, Mary and Joseph took the Baby to the Temple in Jerusalem to present Him to the Lord. As they were walking into the outer court of the Temple, an old man of Jerusalem, named Simeon, hurried up to them and took the Baby in his arms, and began to speak loudly and tearfully to the Lord God. Clutching the Child to his thin old breast, he cried: "Now lettest Thou Thy servant depart in peace, Lord, in agreement with Thy word, for mine eyes have seen Thy salvation, which Thou has prepared before all the nations, a light for revelation to the gentiles, and a glory to Thy people Israel."

Mary and Joseph could only stand and stare at him,

trying to fathom what he said to God. One thing they knew: someone had actually recognized Him! He had called the Baby the Lord's *salvation*. Here in the breast of an ancient stranger, they found another heart which God had prepared for the coming of Mary's Baby. Old Simeon knew Him at once.

When Joseph talked to the old man, he learned that the Holy Spirit had told him that he would not see death before he had actually *seen* the Lord's Messiah!

Simeon blessed them before they left the Temple that day, but he added to the already overwhelming store of things which Mary must ponder in her heart. To Mary herself, he said: "See, this Child is appointed for the falling and rising up of many in Israel and for a sign that shall be contradicted!"

Mary's slight frown as she strained to understand did not stop him. "And a sword shall pass through your soul, so that the reasonings of many hearts may be revealed."

Joseph stepped nearer to where Mary stood with the Baby in her arms. A frown of perplexity furrowed his kind brow, too. What could old Simeon have meant by a sword that would pass through Mary's soul? And how would it reveal the reasonings of many hearts?

That same day in the Temple someone else recognized Him; this time an old woman named Anna, a widow in her eighties, who in her youth had known only seven years of married happiness with her husband before his death. For all the remaining years of her long life, she had lived and served in the Temple of God, worshiping Him day and night. When Anna recognized Jesus, she gave thanks to the Lord and talked about Him to all the people standing around.

Mary could only ponder all these things in her heart and try to learn from them. She and Joseph left the Temple that day in silence. There was too much happening for mere talk, even between two people who loved each other as they did.

* * *

One shining truth must have come clear to both Joseph and Mary that day in the Temple in Jerusalem. It can also come clear to us. Both the old people who had recognized the Baby had spent their lives in communication with the Lord God Himself. Both were so familiar with the very character of God that they noticed the family resemblance in His Son at once. They had both learned to trust His Spirit, and that Spirit witnessed to them instantly when they saw the humble Jewish couple with the Child in the Temple.

Mary must have learned still another great truth from the widow, Anna; one she would have a golden chance to use when her beloved Joseph died after Jesus was in His teens. Anna had not fallen into the pit of self-pity when her married happiness ended at seven years. Instead, she gave herself totally to the worship and service of the Lord God, and now she was rewarded by her own recognition of His Son, the promised Messiah.

But what of the strange words spoken by old Simeon? Surely, neither Mary nor Joseph could make much sense of them. Especially the sword that would pass through Mary's soul. Was her Baby not the Son of God Himself? Hadn't He come to save Israel? Wasn't He going to redeem His people from their sins? Wouldn't this be a glorious, joy-filled thing? A sword passing through a woman's soul meant tragedy, pain, sorrow. How could the Messiah's coming bring sorrow and pain? Neither of them could imagine. And so they left the Temple in silence, their thoughts too confused for talk. But their faith was strengthened, because up to that time, there had only been the shepherds to talk to about him. The shepherds had heard the heavenly announcement first hand, and this had surely lessened their aloneness that night in crowded Bethlehem. But now, here were two more people who knew Him! Mary and Joseph could only let their questions rest in silence and trust in the Lord God.

With the Child had come all of Life to Mary, and all of Life contains sorrow as well as joy. This she knew, but she could not know that for her, the coming of this Life would sweep the wide arc from the first blinding joy when He was born, to the last blinding grief as she watched Him die.

Mary could not have known about the future, as we cannot know, but she knew, and we can know, that with Him comes all of Love. Mary loved her son, and because of the caliber of the love He gave her, she would be ready for the day when He would be forced to *demonstrate* Holy Love to the world, at her expense as well as His own.

Mary's Son and The Sanhedrin

Mary smiled and waved and chatted happily with the

friends and relatives who, group by group, joined the long
caravan of pilgrims on their way over the rough roads,
from Nazareth south through the otherwise forbidden land
of the Samaritans toward the Jordan River. Except for the
annual trip to Jerusalem for the Feast of the Passover,
these people never saw each other. It was a glad time, and
to Mary it always seemed so fitting that they should be
privileged to give thanks to the Lord God in the Holy City
itself, at the end of the journey. She enjoyed seeing the
other children grow up year after year, and exchanged
woman talk with their mothers, accepting their compli-
ments about her fine, sturdy Son, Jesus, who took His
twelve-year-old responsibilities so seriously.

On this trip, she was trying hard to understand her Son's
thoughts. He had never seen Jerusalem before, but now He
was twelve, and His excitement struck Mary as running far
deeper than the usual anticipation of a twelve-year-old
Jewish boy making his first trip to the Holy City.

"It is as though He knows He is going to *His* Father's
house," she mused. Then she tried to rejoin the chatter of
the other women, and found it difficult, so deep was her
feeling for this Boy, so perplexing her thoughts. But she
carried her perplexity uncomplainingly, beneath her great
joy in Jesus.

He was such an obedient Son, never causing her the
anxiety other boys sometimes caused their mothers, just by
being boys. Jesus was an accomplished scholar, and Mary
wasn't at all surprised when He walked for hours alone in
the streets, that first night, after they crossed the Jordan
and covered the fourteen mile climb to Jerusalem. He
would have to see for Himself, this she knew. He would
have to let His fine, young mind roam back through the
centuries, picking out this and that spot in the Holy City so
much a part of His heritage.

But this was as far as Mary could go with Him, as He
walked alone through the narrow, crooked streets. She
could not have known that His heart filled with a strange,
ancient emotion as He stood on the gentle slope of the
Mount of Olives, and looked and looked across the brook
Kidron, toward the great, gold dome of the Temple of
God. Jesus was only twelve, but His heart could experience
antiquity, too. On the day of the Passover, "at even, at the
going down of the sun, at the season that thou camest
forth from Egypt," Jesus ate the Paschal lamb thoughtfully
with Mary and Joseph, and the next day, the caravan of

friends and relatives from Nazareth and Jericho assembled at an appointed place to start the trip back home.

The *dragoman,* the man who went ahead to find lodgings for the night, had already gone. The pack animals were ready, and slowly the line of people passed down the fourteen miles from Jerusalem toward the Jordan River. Mary talked with her friends, and Joseph with his. She had never had to worry about Jesus, so they traveled all day that first day before she began to wonder about Him. Slipping away from her friends, she found Joseph.

"Where is He, Joseph? Have you seen Jesus today?"

Joseph suggested the Boy had probably gone on to help the dragoman; it would be like Him.

"The dragoman came back an hour ago! It's almost time to stop for the night. I'm worried about Him, Joseph."

Joseph walked the length of the line of travelers, asking everyone he met. No one had seen the Boy all day.

In genuine alarm, Joseph and Mary turned back and hurried toward Jerusalem. When they arrived the next day, still with no trace of Him, they were both nearly frantic with worry. Some harm must have come to Him. It was not like Jesus to cause them trouble.

All the third day they went from house to house where someone might know Him, and as the sun began to drop in the high cloudless sky, Mary felt her heart drop, too, with its load of anxiety.

"The Temple, Mary! We haven't looked for Him at the Temple yet. The house of God holds a real attraction for the Boy. We'll go there."

Joseph supported Mary as they hurried toward the Temple where at the close of the Passover festival, the educated, scholarly members of the Sanhedrin had descended from their lofty quarters to the lower levels of the Temple to hold public discussion.

Joseph steered Mary through the curious, jostling crowd gathered around the members of the Sanhedrin, seated a little apart in a circle of richly brocaded robes and jeweled turbans. Joseph peered over the crowd anxiously, and there, quietly sitting with the high governing body, was Jesus.

"There He is, Mary! He's sitting right down with the Teachers, conversing with them like one of their body. They're listening to the Boy, too."

Mary couldn't take this in. She was only filled with relief that they had found Him at last, and wept softly and thanked God, as she waited for Joseph to bring Him to her. When Joseph and Jesus and Mary had pushed their way out of the crowd to the outer court of the Temple, the Boy said nothing at all to them. He was not rebellious at having been interrupted, nor did He seem fearful that they would scold him. He simply waited respectfully for them to speak first.

Mary, somewhat recovered from her worry, said what any mother might have said to her son: "Child, why have You treated us this way? Your father and I have been anxiously looking for You!"

Joseph couldn't resist a little fatherly pride in what he had seen. "But Mary, you should have heard the way He was talking to those scholars. And they paid attention to Him, too. They respected Him."

Being a woman, Mary was still nervous, and although her pride rivaled Joseph's, she just had to add: "Nevertheless, Joseph, we were worried sick about the Boy. Child, why have you treated us this way?"

Jesus neither smiled nor frowned. He simply looked at her and asked in His steady boy's voice, "Why were you seeking Me? Did you not know that I ought to be about My Father's affairs?"

For a moment this serious faced Boy of twelve might have been their parent. Neither of them understood what He had just said; but neither of them said anything more.

He went home with them cheerfully and obediently, and back in Nazareth, He lived the remainder of His youthful years honoring and obeying both Mary and Joseph as He had always done.

*   *   *

Mary now had still more to ponder in her heart, still more to add to her perplexity, but for all the years He remained at home in Nazareth, He kept adding to her joy, too.

This incident at the Temple in Jerusalem has little to offer the modern mother in the area of child discipline. No woman ever had a Child like Jesus, Mary's Son. We are told that He grew in wisdom and in stature and in favor with the people who knew Him, but from the beginning there had been a kind of sane balance about this Boy which bred reverence in His mother's mind and heart.

It seems important here, however, to see that He apparently did not make her feel unnatural with Him. He was the Son of God, but He was also Mary's Son. Her reactions when she thought He was lost, were the same as any mother would have under the circumstances. She even scolded Him a little outside the Temple, after they found Him. Scolded Him, half in relief and half in annoyance. Until they found Him, she felt only anxiety over His safety. But once they did find Him, she resorted to the utterly human mother-reaction, and began to be somewhat overcome with all the trouble His absence had caused.

That she respected His human dignity, every mother should observe, but more important to us today is that Mary's Son was God in the flesh. And God never causes us to feel stiff or unnatural with Him! The relationship between Mary and her Boy was the closest possible human relationship, and you and I can be as close to Him today as we want to be. If He did not make His own Mother feel unnatural, as she tried day in and day out to be what He needed her to be, why should we feel unnatural with Him now?

Jesus was a growing Boy at the time of this incident, but He was also God on earth, moving among his people—human beings with weakness and personality quirks like our own. Not once did He compromise His holiness in order to grow in favor with the people around Him, but neither did He show any indication of trying to make them uncomfortable or ill at ease with Him.

Mary's Son is the God we worship now. And He longs for us to be at home with Him, as He intended us to be when He created us in the first place.

"Come unto Me, and I will rest you," He said. We all rest only when we are being ourselves, when we are natural.

If you and I can honestly say we are more at home with God than anyone else on earth, then we can know we are beginning, at least, to know Him as He really is.

Jesus and His Mother Attend a Wedding

After Joseph's death a few years later, Jesus took full charge of the carpentry shop and His mother. She loved to watch Him, grown tall now and wide shouldered, stride from their house each morning toward the shop, a heavy beam of oak or cedar balanced on His shoulder. She was proud of Him and felt utterly secure with Him to care for

her. He had helped her live through the grief-filled, empty
days without Joseph. He was her life. But she had never
become overly dependent upon Him. This was God's Son,
and surely God needed Him for more than to care for a
Hebrew woman named Mary of Nazareth.

And then one day He left and never came back to live
with her in the little house on the Nazareth hillside again.
Mary didn't see her Son until after His baptism by her
cousin Elizabeth's son, John; until after He had quietly
begun His ministry in Galilee. In fact, they met again for
the first time, as far as we know, at a wedding Mary attended in Cana, a lovely small village spread on the gentle
slope of a hill, a few miles from Nazareth. She had no idea
her Son, Jesus, would be there. But in He walked, just
before the wedding feast began, followed by Mary's two
nephews, James and John, and four other men whom she
didn't know. After He embraced her, He introduced her to
Peter and Andrew, who were fishermen, and their friends,
Nathaniel and Philip. These were His disciples, but He
didn't tell her so Himself. The men were so excited, they
told her all about it. They were all prepared to leave their
homes and families if necessary to follow Him anywhere
He led them.

Mary's heart ran over with joy and wonder, but still she
felt comfortable and natural with Him, and as the feast
progressed, she did a most natural thing.

"Jesus," she whispered over His shoulder as He reclined
at the table with His disciples, "I have just learned that
they are out of wine!"

To expect Him to be able to do something about this
emergency situation was as natural to Mary as breathing.
He had never let her down on anything. Now she was asking Him to do something about relieving the embarrass-
ment of their friends before all the invited guests.

His answer was a strange one—strange to us, until we
think it through. But His voice was kind when He said,
"Woman, what is that between Me and you? My hour is
not here yet!"

He was not trying to humiliate her. Jesus knew His
mother and knew that a social emergency like this genuinely upset her. She was a hostess, too, and felt keen
identity with her friends. At that moment, Mary must have
both understood and misunderstood Him. From the first
she had understood and misunderstood so much about
Him. Still she stood waiting before Him, because she had

always had such confidence in Him. She said no more to her Son, she did not argue, but simply instructed the waiter to do whatever Jesus told him to do.

What He had said Mary simply left alone to think on later, but she acted normally, still trusting Him to do something. And He did. He ordered the six water jars used for the Jewish rite of purifying to be filled with water. The waiters filled them all the way to the brim. Then Jesus ordered them to dip out some of the contents of the jars and take it to the table manager. His disciples must have enjoyed the look on the manager's face when he tasted the sudden supply of excellent wine. Mary must have smiled happily, too, satisfied now that the crisis had ended, but not at all surprised that Jesus had ended it as He did, by turning ordinary well water into the choicest wine.

*　　　*　　　*

What did Jesus really mean when He spoke those strange words to His mother at the wedding in Cana? She had asked an ordinary favor of Him. I doubt that she expected Him to perform His first public miracle as He did, but she had grown accustomed to depending upon Him, and so, when the emergency arose, she went to Him simply, the way a child would run to its father for help.

"Woman, what is that between Me and you? My hour is not here yet!"

What did He mean? Certainly Mary did not know, but the strangeness of His words in no way altered her faith in Him. All these centuries have passed and still we do not know all that He meant, but it is generally agreed that He was making His first attempt to tell her that the intimate period of their close, personal, family relationship was coming to an end. He loved her no less, but He was now more than her Son, He was her God. He would be her Saviour, too. Because He had become utterly human, although He remained God, this must have been difficult for Him, too. But it is quite plain, if we really think it through, that He was not refusing His mother's request. Did the Son of God change His mind in a flash just to please her? He did not. He possessed the mind of God from the beginning. His mother certainly did not cause Him to weaken in the overall purpose of His ministry just begun. He was simply trying to use this homely, daily incident as an illustration to help her understand that their relationship was now broadening, that He now belonged to the world, as well as to her. When Mary failed to understand, He, of course, supplied the wine. Or—perhaps Mary did not fail to understand. We have no more recorded conversation between them at Cana, but at any rate, He was talking about a much wider issue than merely supplying the needed wine for a wedding feast.

It is extremely interesting and encouraging to me that in the face of the sweeping excitement and purpose of His beginning ministry, He bothered to attend to a social amenity such as this. He bothered to care about a seemingly little thing. Why did He do this? Because He was God, and this is what God is like.

Whether Mary fully grasped His meaning is really not important here. What is important is that the strange speech did not stop her faith in Him! She simply turned and quietly gave the waiter an order, still expecting Jesus to come through.

God may seem to be saying strange, unfamiliar things to us now and then, when we approach Him for help, as Mary did that day. Does it stop us? Is our faith dependent upon our understanding of His words? Or is it dependent upon what we know of Him?

Mary depended upon her Son because of what she had learned about Him through their years together. We can do this, too. True faith is the *natural result* of knowing what God is like. It is never dependent upon our being able to understand all that He may be trying to say to us.

Closed in by Pain

Months went by in which Mary had no chance even to glimpse her son, Jesus, as He moved from city to city with His disciples, teaching and healing the enormous crowds of people who thronged Him wherever He went. He had urged her to move to Capernaum, which was His headquarters during the first months of His earthly ministry, and of course, she heard the ugly rumors about Him. Her son, James, irritated by the publicity Jesus received, caused Mary to remember often what old Simeon had said about the sword that would pass through her soul. She loved all her sons, and it grieved her that James and the others failed to understand Jesus. Once they had persuaded her to go with them to try to stop Him; after all, people were saying He was devil-possessed, and this fantastic practice of healing lame men on the Sabbath was hurting His brothers' reputation for being solid, sensible businessmen. She went along, and waiting at the edge of the pressing crowd outside the synagogue where He had just healed a man, she felt the "sword" once more, when He sent word back that His mother and His brothers were *all* who followed God! Mary did not fully understand what He meant; she was hurt not to be received by Him, but she trusted Him still. He had a reason for saying what He said. Mary had never fully understood her son, but she had never stopped believing in Him. She felt the natural hurt in her mother heart at being separated from Him, but she kept clear in her mind that this beloved Son of hers was also the Son of God. In her heart, Mary wanted Him to be about His Father's business.

He was about that business day in and day out, for almost three action-packed years, and then she began to hear the most frightening news of all. The rulers of the Jews, the governing body who had received Him with such interest in the Temple when He was twelve, now had turned against Him. They believed Him to be a heretic. To their legalistic minds Jesus had set Himself above the Lord God of Israel. From place to place, they followed Him and attempted to trap Him into admitting His heresy. As he eluded them or stopped their tirades with wisdom beyond their merely human minds, the anger in their hearts increased.

"They'll crucify Him," James had said one day. "It's against Jewish law for the Sanhedrin to do it, but those wise men will find a way! He's gone too far."

Mary remembered the "sword" again and prayed fervently for protection for her Son.

Then it was Passover time, and although Mary knew He would be unable to eat the Paschal lamb with her, she allowed her mind to go back to His first trip with her and Joseph to Jerusalem when He was twelve. She felt much of the same sickening anxiety in her heart for Him most of the time now that she and Joseph had felt during the three days in which they had searched for Jesus all over Jerusalem so many years ago. He was thirty-three, and the most talked about Man in Judea, but He was still her Boy.

The days dragged by, and Mary felt more and more isolated in her growing fear and anxiety. Her isolation was not unlike those first few days after the Angel had told her He was coming. But Elizabeth had been dead a long time now, and although Mary of Magdala, from whom Jesus had cast seven devils, was a loyal and faithful friend, the younger woman needed Mary to comfort her, so great was her own anxiety for His safety. Salome, the mother of Jesus' favorite disciple, John, was a good friend, too. But Mary's isolation increased because no other woman on earth could be expected to know the mingling pride and anguish and confusion in her heart.

And then the dread news reached her at last. Jesus had been betrayed by Judas, His strange, lean-faced, high-strung disciple. Mary felt His pain over Judas, too. Now, she was all pain. Her isolation was complete.

Of all people on earth, Mary knew He was God's Son. But now God's Son was surely going to die.

*   *   *

When the Angel of the Lord first came to Mary to announce Jesus' Birth, the young, simple Jewish girl experienced the isolation of pure joy. The human heart is not made for isolation, however, and so she had hurried to her cousin, Elizabeth, needing someone to share her joy.

Now she was isolated by pain. Who would bear this with her? She was able to find out only snatches of what had actually happened to Him during the long, terrible night in which He had been dragged by ropes from Pilate to Herod and back to Pilate again after His arrest. Someone said He was being tried early in the morning. Were His disciples with Him? All except Judas? Surely they were, she thought; and then John, His beloved disciple, had burst into his mother Salome's house, where Mary sat waiting, and wept so bitterly that Mary comforted the young man as best she could. She loved John. After all, this sensitive boy had seemed to love Jesus with all his heart.

"I didn't love Him enough!" John sobbed. "I ran, too—like all the rest of them."

"John," Mary's voice was old and hoarse. "John, did no one stay with Him?"

"No one," John had said.

The guilty disciple talked on but Mary didn't hear. Now, there was only the pain around her once more.

She knew He would be crucified. Her pure, sinless, kind, love-filled Son was going to be executed on a criminal's cross, while the people watched.

The final word had not yet come, but Mary must have

known. How did she face it? How was she able to move about a room? To carry on even fragments of conversation? How was it that she didn't die literally of pain during these long, tormented moments as she waited to know the details?

Perhaps she began to gain some measure of self-control by deliberately questioning John further. Did Peter leave Him, too? John's brother, James? Matthew, for whom He had done so much? All of them? All of them. He was alone now somewhere out in the cruel, curious city—the Holy City turned evil this night. Alone, with His enemies all around Him.

What held Mary's heart from total destruction now? The Lord God. Slowly she must have repeated His name. "Lord God of Israel, be with Him now." Slowly she turned her own pain away. Jesus' pain was all that mattered now. Whatever she could do as His mother, she must do now. She no longer mattered. Her isolation melted down and she moved out of it toward Him, wherever He was. Mary moved with all her spiritual strength toward her Son, and as she moved, the Lord God of Israel moved with her.

Perhaps, after awhile, she turned to John and said: "We will be at His cross with Him, John. Dry your tears, boy, He will need us now as never before. We will be at His cross with Him."

No woman's pain was ever more complete than Mary's, but she took God's strength to move her attention away from her own anguish toward the anguish of the One she loved above every other person on earth. This is possible for us, if it was possible for her. Her Son has hung on His cross now, and we can know in retrospect, that power enough was released that dark day, to move us away from our own pain into a creative action toward our own loved ones.

Pain is still pain, but God is still God. We only need to be willing, as Mary was willing, to look away from our pain toward love. And once we look, He will give us the inner power to act on what we see.

Mary's Sword and Her Son's Cross

Mary and John stood at the foot of His cross, closed in by the terrible heat, the shrieks of agony from the two thieves hanging on either side of Him, the shouts of ridicule from the curious mob.

"He saved others," one of the fat priests of the Temple screamed. "Now, let him save himself! If he is the Christ of God, the chosen one—let him save himself!"

Did Jesus see them standing there? They both prayed He did. *If only it could help Him a little, knowing they were there.*

John's guilt was hotter than the relentless sun. How had he been able to run just when the Master needed someone to stand by Him? Did it help now, knowing John alone of all the others, had come to the cross? What was He thinking as He hung there? Did He see them? Would even He be able to forgive John for his cowardice the night before?

"Father, forgive them, for they know not what they do."

Mary clutched John's arm. "Did you hear what He said, John?"

"Yes, I heard. It's as though He read my thoughts just now. Not only does He forgive me, but these—these fiends here, too!"

John's arm tightened about Mary's frail shoulders. He felt quieter now, stronger. He was experiencing forgiveness, even as he stared horrified at the cost of that forgiveness to his Master who loved him.

Only one hour had passed. Mary refused John's suggestion that they move a distance away. "I'm afraid He can't see me back there, John." She could only whisper now, but Mary seemed unaware of herself at all. The moments edged by, between her stinging memories. His blood trickled to the dry, hard earth from His dear feet nailed to the rough upright of the cross. Mary thought about how His feet used to look, slender, strong, covered with dust from running down the road in the evening back in Nazareth, as soon as He saw her lamp flare in the high front window of their home. Dear, dear days. Good, work-filled, natural, happy days. Gone, with Joseph. Now, with Him. Now. Now He hung there, her Son. God's Son. *God's Son.*

Mary raised her eyes from the darkening drops on the ground. Yes! He was God's Son. He was even now, even in public disgrace, about His Father's business.

John was talking. What was he saying? "That last night, the Master said, 'Let not your hearts be troubled.' "

"He said that, John?"

"Yes—He seemed to make a point of it."

"What else did He say that night? Think, John!"

"He said, 'Let not your hearts be troubled; you believe in God, believe also in Me!' "

Mary's thirsty heart drank John's words and grew quiet. She listened intently to the young disciple beside her, but she looked full into the face of her Son.

"Let not your hearts be troubled . . . In my Father's house are many homes. If this were not so, I *would* have told you."

It was as though Jesus spoke to her now: "I go away to prepare a place for you, and when I have gone and have prepared a place for you, I will come again and take you along with Me, so that where I am, you also will be."

"He will do that, John! If He said that, He will come again and take us along with Him." For a moment, her heart, even her hope rose, then sorrow and weariness overcame her. And as though He knew this there in His agony, Jesus Himself began to speak.

"Closer, John! We must move closer—He's saying something to us."

"*Woman—behold your son!*" Slowly, agonizingly, He managed to bend His head toward John. "*John—behold your mother!*"

Even as His words lifted their hearts above their human grief, He took care to reach toward them with this tender, human gesture of love. He would lift their hearts, as their God and Saviour, but He would also give them to each other to be mother and son to share earthly joys and comforts, when He was no longer with them.

*   *   *

As God had given Him to Mary to be her Son for a little while on earth, now He was giving John to her to help fill the emptiness in her life during her remaining years.

His words to the disciples the night they shared their last supper with Him, lifted their hearts from the perplexity and sorrow of His going, toward eternity. The very God of that eternity had become one of the people of earth for awhile, and now He was returning to His Father to prepare a place for His loved ones. There would never be darker hours on earth than those hours while Mary and John stood watching His life drain away. *But* He was leaving with a purpose, and His purpose was directed toward them. Toward us, too.

Dimly at first, then more clearly, He helped Mary see that her Son's painful death was not going to be wasted! He was going to prepare a place for her, for John, for the others who followed Him—for us. To hear the words, "Let not your hearts be troubled . . ." when our hearts are breaking, can seem a mockery, *unless* we know the One who dared to say them! Mary knew Him. John knew Him. They both received comfort. So can we, *if* we know Him personally.

But does He expect us to "let not our hearts be troubled" merely by well intentioned self-effort and an attempt at a sudden burst of new faith? Not at all. Just as He did with Mary and John at the cross, so He will do with us, when He sees that our hearts need help in the dark, anguished moments. Even as He lifted their faith, He also recognized their suffering that fearful afternoon on the little hill outside the Holy City. And recognizing it, *He did something to alleviate it.* He remembered that they were only human beings, and that they had long years of human life to live out on this earth. He bothered, in the midst of His agony, to make the bridge for them, from the *human* to the *divine.* His death was not useless, He had made its purpose as clear as their understanding demanded, but then He did something definite to help them take their first faltering steps across the bridge from having loved Him humanly, to loving Him as God: He gave them to each other!

He has not changed. God, in Jesus Christ, is the same today as He was that afternoon at Golgotha. He is still ready to lift our hearts toward heaven, but He is also still mindful of our human needs. God has not changed. He is still intent upon *giving* to us. Our part is to be willing to receive.

He Came Back at Pentecost

Mary had seen the Angel with her own eyes. Along with Mary of Magdala and Salome, she had gone early on the first day of the new week, to prepare His dear, broken Body which they had seen placed in the fine hillside grave of Joseph of Arimathea.

The women found the stone rolled away, and there was the Angel, announcing to them that Mary's Son, Jesus, had risen from the dead! Her heart had been too full of pure

joy to register surprise, too. After all, Mary had lived all of
the years of her earthly life since His Birth, growing
familiar with His uniqueness. This Son of hers had never
been like other boys; only *He* was God's Son, too.

She was shocked to find His Body gone, but Mary had
believed the Lord's Angel before Jesus was born. She
believed him now. She was genuinely sorry that Peter and
John and the others wouldn't believe dear Mary Magdalene
when she ran to tell them of His Resurrection, but the
years had made her wise. They would believe it eventually.
Jesus would do something to help them believe.

Now, she had been sitting in the upper room in the
home of Mark's mother for over a week, waiting. With her
were the remaining eleven disciples, (Judas had killed himself in shame), and well over a hundred other people who
had followed Him on earth. Mary smiled a little as she
looked affectionately on the other women, now welcome in
the once select group. James and John and Peter and Andrew and the others were no longer feeling superior; they
had all behaved too badly when He was arrested that night
in the garden. They welcomed even the women now, on
equal terms.

But most welcome to the group waiting there in the upper room, at least to Mary, were her other sons, whom
James had brought into faith in Jesus at last. James had always been so antagonistic toward Him during His earthly
ministry. James was a leader, a great talker, a dogmatic
fellow, though a good man in his way. Mary smiled again,
remembering how right it had been for Jesus to have appeared alone to James, after His Resurrection. He knew
James was the key to His other brothers, and He had been
right.

Now they were all there, waiting because He had told
them to wait. Mary's presence was a source of great
strength to the others. She was going to have something of
her beloved Son back again! He said His Spirit would come
to give them power to begin a totally new phase of His
work; they would have "power from on high." And then
He had actually said, "I, Myself, will come." No one,
including Mary, understood all of what He meant, but He
had never let her down. If He said He would come, He
would come. However He came to them, it would be right
and it would be Jesus, and for her that was enough.

Eight days passed, and then nine. It was once more the
Feast of Pentecost. Jerusalem was never so crowded as at

this time of year, when good sailing enabled Jews from all countries of the known world to assemble at the Holy City for the great feast day. Through the ancient streets the world met itself, as men and women laughed and jostled and talked together. There were Parthians, Medes, Elamites, Mesopotamians, Judeans, travelers from Cappadocia, Pontus, Asia, Phrygia, Pamphylia, Egypt, Cyrene, Rome, Crete and Arabia. All of them spoke either Greek or Aramaic during their stay in Jerusalem, although almost every known language was represented, as residents from the same localities met and visited together.

The clatter and confusion from the streets drifted up and through the open windows of the upper room where the one hundred and twenty waited for Him to keep His promise to them. They waited mostly in silence, as they prayed together as one. They were there early on the morning of the day of Pentecost, but their waiting that day was short-lived. A little before nine o'clock, the sunlit Holy City was struck suddenly by what appeared to be a great wind—so strong the people fled the streets, crowding into shops and inns to escape the blowing dust and debris.

There was no rain and no darkness, only the great roaring from heaven. It filled the upper room where the disciples waited, and over the head of each of the others, Mary, His mother, saw tiny flames appear; flames that separated, then danced a moment, as one after another was filled with the promised Holy Spirit, and began to speak and praise God in foreign languages!

Suddenly Mary was released forever from her human perplexity over why God had chosen her to be His mother; released and relieved now to be what she had always felt she wanted to be, just another one of His followers. Her special mission was over, and along with the rest, her new life in Christ Jesus had begun. Out into the street she went rejoicing with her friends, speaking right along with them, in the native language of everyone she met, concerning the fact of the risen Christ!

*   *   *

Mary's special mission ended that day. Even the dark grief she had carried in her heart was gone. He had come back. The Spirit who filled each of them that day was not a strange, new Spirit. They all felt at home—more at home than ever before in their entire lives! The only new aspect was the power that now dwelt within each one. Even this did not seem strange, nor make them feel set apart and special. It made them feel an integral part of Him, of His universe, of His world. They felt His longings and shared His desires for each human being on earth. They were now at home with the power they had tried so hard to imitate when He had lived among them.

Mary must have experienced intense relief! Every minute of her life as His mother had been treasured, but there had been so much to ponder in her heart; so much she didn't understand. Now, since she, too, had been filled with His Spirit, she no longer felt set apart in a way she couldn't understand. She felt even more needed, but her heart was quiet now, and what she couldn't understand no longer disturbed her. Mary was a simple, humble Hebrew woman, who had been somewhat ill at ease with such a famous Son. Her heart sang loudly that day, because as much as she had always loved this Son of hers, now, she found she was free to love Him even more, and in tempo and harmony with all the others.

What a travesty on the gift of God's Spirit, when we suddenly feel "special" or particularly "set up" over receiving it! Christendom is being divided and scarred by misunderstanding and unconscious cruelty from those who feel they have been given the Gift of the Spirit in some particular way. This unrest and confusion is growing daily, until God's people more resemble the crowds jostling on the streets of Jerusalem that Pentecost Day than the suddenly sane and balanced Christians who poured joyfully from the upper room to attract five thousand new believers at once.

We need to think deeply here. His Spirit is offered to everyone who believes Him. If His coming manifests itself in some unusual way to some, does it mean that His Spirit has altered? Jesus Christ was all sanctity when He was on earth, but He was also all *sanity*. He said, "I, Myself, will come." Would He change His own personality? No. Whatever outward manifestations of the Spirit may appear in your personality, the *only one* safe to depend upon is the Spirit of Love. Whether you speak in tongues, or heal the sick, or expound the Scriptures, or preach—*do you love?* Are you more humble? Or are you feeling superior?

God had asked Mary for a special, holy use of her life, and she gave herself willingly. But when the Spirit of her Son came at the Jewish Feast of Pentecost that day so long ago, Mary was still being called by God, this time to an equally holy place, but with her He also called all the others who would listen. Mary was relieved once more to be like her friends.

Is this what we want today? Are we glad just to be members of the human race called by God Himself? Or do we feel so special that we are not comfortable unless we are expounding or speaking from a platform or healing the sick or worshiping God in unknown tongues?

All of these things can come from Him; this is not the point here. Our part is to keep ourselves concentrating not upon which special gifts *we* have received, but on the sane, balanced, Holy Giver, Himself.

16. ELIZABETH

A Woman Free From Doubt

The small donkey on which young Mary rode from Jerusalem, where she had stopped overnight on her journey from Nazareth, plodded slowly up the lane to her cousin Elizabeth's house in the hills outside the Holy City. Mary hoped secretly that Elizabeth would be alone, knowing this was not likely since the old lady had given all the years of her childless life to the needs of her neighbors who worshiped God in the Temple where her husband, Zacharias, was a priest.

There was no one in the courtyard of her cousin's house, though, and Mary grew more hopeful. Then in the doorway stood Elizabeth, tall, erect, in a cheerful blue dress, the hot afternoon wind whipping the pink veil which covered her gray hair.

"Elizabeth!"

The young Hebrew girl dismounted quickly and ran toward her aging cousin, and as she drew near, the old woman's face lighted and she clasped her unborn child who leaped suddenly within her.

"Oh, Mary," Elizabeth called in a strong, glad voice. "Blessed are you among women and blessed is the fruit of your womb!"

Mary had told her nothing. Elizabeth knew by the Holy Spirit that this young cousin of hers was going to give birth to the Messiah! Elizabeth's long life had been a devout one; the promise of the coming Messiah had filled her heart since childhood. She had grieved at being childless, but now even this grief was gone. The same Angel who appeared to Mary, had already appeared to old Zacharias in the Temple. Elizabeth had no need to waste time with exchanging stories or asking questions. She had never doubted God. Certainly this was no time to begin.

With great confidence and certainty, the humble, devout old woman remarked: "And how did this happen to me, that my Lord's mother should visit me?"

"You know already, Elizabeth?" Mary wasn't idly

curious, either. Eternity was at work through these two women.

"You do know already!"

"Yes, Mary—when the voice of your greeting reached my ears just now, the babe leaped within me for joy! And blessed are you who believed that the things told her by the Lord shall be accomplished."

"I do believe, cousin. I *know*. I do not understand, but I know. The Angel of the Lord told me also about your baby. I did not come merely to see it with my own eyes—I came because it is all so strange, and I needed to talk first with you." Mary lifted her young, round face to the blue, cloudless sky and rejoiced. "It is not that I am troubled, cousin. My soul magnifies the Lord and my spirit is glad in God my Saviour, for He took notice of the lowliness of His servant girl. See, from now on all generations will call me blessed, for the Almighty has done great things for me; His name is holy and His mercy is on those who reverence Him through all generations."

Mary's aloneness vanished. Elizabeth was in it now with her. The two women shared strength and joy and expectation. Over and over they relived the things which had already taken place.

Zacharias, Elizabeth's husband, could not converse with Mary; he had been unable to speak since the Angel Gabriel had appeared to him that evening in the Temple, as he lighted the incense pot before offering prayers for the people clustered outside. Mary learned the story from Elizabeth: "Suddenly the Angel was there beside my husband, standing just to the right of the altar of incense. Zacharias was filled with fear, but the Angel said to him, 'Have no fear, Zacharias, because your prayer has been heard; your wife Elizabeth will bear you a son, whom you will call John. He will afford you joy and happiness and many shall be glad at his birth; for he shall be great before the Lord. He shall drink no wine or liquor at all, and from his birth he shall be filled with the Holy Spirit. Many of the sons of Israel shall he turn to the Lord their God, before whom he shall go forth in the spirit and power of Elijah, to turn the hearts of the fathers to the children and the obstinate to the wisdom of the righteous, to prepare a people that is ready for the Lord.'

"Zacharias painstakingly wrote it all down so that I could know all that the Angel of the Lord said to him that evening. My dear husband *was* afraid, though, Mary," the old woman said gently. "He was troubled and asked of the Angel: 'In what way can I be assured of this, for I am an old man and my wife is advanced in years?' "

"Was it really doubt, Elizabeth—or merely fear?"

"Perhaps they are close in meaning, Mary. It is sometimes difficult for a man with an inquiring mind like Zacharias to be a little child even before the Lord whom he loves so much. At any rate, the Angel replied: 'I am Gabriel, who stands in the presence of God, and I was sent to speak to you and to announce these glad tiding to you.' And when Zacharias tried to answer and was dumb, the Angel of the Lord said, 'Observe! You will be silent and unable to speak until the day when these things take place, because thou didst not believe my words, which shall come true at the proper time.' " Old Elizabeth smiled compassionately, thinking how difficult it had been all these six months and more for her husband to be unable to talk! "Do you wonder the day you came, Mary, that I said, 'Blessed is she who believed that the things told her by the Lord shall be accomplished'?"

Mary stayed with Elizabeth for three months, until the baby came. And once more she saw still another sign that God's plan was being carried out step by step, on schedule. The happy, laughing friends and relatives who gathered in Zacharias' home of course thought the new baby would be named for his father.

"No," Elizabeth said. "The Angel of the Lord said his name was to be called John."

Zacharias wrote on a piece of parchment: "His name is John." From that moment on, the old man could speak again. And he rejoiced and praised God, and his wife and their cousin, Mary, and all their friends.

*   *   *

I doubt that God was actually punishing old Zacharias for having doubted. It is just as plausible that He was merely going the second mile in order to strengthen his faith. After all, the Angel did tell the old priest that he would not speak until the Word of the Lord had been fulfilled. The Word of the Lord was fulfilled both from God's side and from the human side, when both the baby's parents insisted that there be a break with tradition where the child's name was concerned. They did not name him for his father, they named him John.

God works with each individual according to what He knows of the individual's needs. He knew Zacharias to be a more complex person than his wife, Elizabeth.

After all, God sent His Angel to the old man, not to his wife. He knew who had the potential doubts. So far as we can learn from the recorded story of Elizabeth, she was one of those rare persons who had no battle with doubts whatever.

She was utterly childlike, utterly open, utterly believing. She was the one through whose body this miracle birth was to take place, but God knew it was her husband who would require the convincing.

There is no indication, however, that old Elizabeth felt superior to her husband simply because she happened to have the kind of nature which can believe quickly. Hers seems to be an authentically generous heart. She drew the comparison between Zacharias' doubts and Mary's faith, but she did not press the point. Apparently the old woman was simply relieved and glad that Mary had been able to believe at once. She allowed her husband's confusion to breed gratitude in her for Mary's simplicity; she did not allow it to breed anything so negative as superiority over Zacharias. Elizabeth seems to have been gifted with true discernment, real objectivity. She accepted her husband's behavior—she accepted her husband *as he was,* not as she might have wished him to be.

Zacharias was a godly man. In the midst of so much known corruption among the priests in charge of the Temple of God just before the Birth of Christ, here was a good man. His wife, of all people, would know whether or not that was true. She knew it was, and she went right on revering this husband of hers for the worth she had found in him through all the long years of their lives together.

She did not mount a spiritual pedestal when suddenly she learned that she was going to be the mother of a baby who would be filled with the Holy Spirit from birth. She did not go about exhibiting her specialties and downgrading Zacharias' weakness, as some women are so prone to do. Elizabeth did have a special visitation from God. This woman was far too old to become pregnant. But it did not increase anything but her humility—before God, before Mary, and before her husband.

She could also have felt some jealousy that her cousin, so much younger than she, was to be the mother of the Messiah, when her son, John, was to be merely the one who would announce the coming of Mary's Son. Elizabeth was not complicated by feelings of superiority or of jealousy. She was balanced, sane, truly humble. Her inner self was not cluttered with non-essentials; and so she could enjoy her son. She kept her heart spacious, with plenty of room for joy.

Could it be that we do not experience more of the joy of knowing God simply because we are poor housekeepers in the rooms of our inner selves? Are these rooms furnished with poor spiritual taste and cluttered with wrong reactions? Are we ignoring our need for inner space?

We can all be filled with the very fullness of God Himself, but we must learn to make room for it as Elizabeth did.

17. HERODIAS

A Woman Who Ruled Her Daughter

Old Elizabeth's son, John the Baptist, sat chained in his narrow, dark cell, cut from the solid rock under Machaerus Fortress. His voice had not been heard proclaiming the Coming Messiah for months now, and his once strong, sunbrowned arms and legs were pale and weakened. He had been thrown into the filthy prison for speaking out against the immoral marriage of Herodias and Herod Antipas.

Herodias hated John with all her passionate, darkened heart. She had never been fully satisfied that her husband had merely imprisoned him. And on a chilly, February night in the year 29, Herodias had her chance for revenge against John. It was the Tetrarch Herod's birthday, and the high vaulted, ornate hall was filled with laughing, drinking guests, all eager for some new excitement to relieve their boredom.

Herod drank deeply from the large crystal cup beside him and leaned back in his hand-carved chair to watch Salome, Herodias' young daughter by her first marriage, as she began to dance for him.

Her long veils furled and billowed about her as her lithe, slim body moved them gracefully and swiftly, like a strong spring wind. The music quickened and her dancing followed its primitive tempo, as the girl dropped one veil after another, the men howling with delight, Herod louder than anyone.

Finally she dropped at his feet, waiting for him to speak.

"Salome, my dear, you danced so magnificently, I will give you whatever you ask me—up to half of my kingdom!"

The girl looked quickly toward her mother, Herodias, who stood behind Herod's big chair. Herod, commenting and laughing drunkenly with his friends, seemed not to miss her for the moment in which she conferred briefly with Herodias.

"What shall I ask of him, Mother?"

Herodias' strong fingers gripped the girl's arm. "This is the hour for which I have lived, Salome! My husband has never agreed to please me by executing that dreadful preacher. Now he will agree to it. He won't want to—he's afraid of the power the Baptist has over these stupid people—but the king is an honorable man. He will keep the promise he made to you. Now, Salome, go back to the king and tell him you want him to give you, this moment, on a plate—the despised head of John the Baptist!"

The girl curtsied to her mother and obeyed her. That night, the big, urgent voice of Elizabeth's son, John, was silenced.

*   *   *

From her own point of view, which was all she had, Herodias had reason to despise John the Baptist. After all, he had been the only one with courage enough to speak out against the king because he had taken his own brother's wife, Herodias. Herod was uncomfortable and angry with John, but he did fear an uprising among John's followers and so had merely imprisoned him and left him to die someday.

Perhaps refusing to execute John had been the first time Herod had crossed his beautiful wife, Herodias. As much as their pagan minds could understand love, they loved each other. At least, Herodias chose ultimate exile with Herod rather than the asylum offered her when he was finally dethroned. Also according to their pagan standards of honor, she knew him to be an honorable man. He had made an offer to Salome, her daughter by Herod's brother, and she knew he would keep his promise. Her quick mind knew, too, that she had made a way for Herod to ease what conscience he might have for John's beheading by giving him a chance to be honorable with Salome.

But all this is relevant only to the personality of Herodias, where we are concerned. Relevant to us, if we care to look for similar traits within ourselves. Although it is not likely that any woman reading this book will be about the business of maneuvering a murder, it is not at all unlikely that there may be one who holds a similar, though somewhat more civilized grip on the mind of her daughter or son or husband. This teen-aged girl, Salome, had known no other life. She had gone with her mother when she left her father to marry Herod. The girl didn't think of asking Herod for something *she* might want, but ran at once to Herodias for instructions. The inevitable weakening of a child's mind so under the control of a parent is obvious in the story of Herodias and her daughter. It may be different in consequence, but it can be just as obviously demonstrated in the twentieth century.

Young people need to learn to make their own decisions, do their own thinking, make their own choices. And no woman should be misled by the seemingly respectable atmosphere of her mental domination of her son or daughter. The end results can be death-like, not to someone else perhaps, but to the very object of the domineering mother's attention—the child herself.

We who live respectable and respected lives, seldom stop to think on the *immorality* involved in using another person to advance our own selfish ends, no matter how "respectable" these ends may appear to be. Mothers "use" their children this way, and although they are almost always unaware of it, the consequences continue to be destructive, because when any human being "uses" another selfishly, there is an issue of immorality involved. When God's moral laws are broken, destruction in some form results. In the case of the mother who presses her own strong opinions and behavior patterns on her child, she contributes to the destruction of the child's moral and mental stability by stealing his character before it has a chance to develop. The submissive son will grow up someday, and if he finds himself unable to make decisions as a man, his wife and his business associates—but mostly he himself—will pay for mother's domination. The daughter will grow up, and when she is unable to keep a firm hand on her own children, they will pay—but so will she, for mother's domination.

It never occurred to Salome to ask for something for herself. She ran to mother for instructions. Her "self" had long ago been buried in Herodias' ego.

18. MARY AND MARTHA

As Different as Day and Night

Martha, the older of the two sisters, owned the house where Jesus perhaps felt more at home than anywhere else during the last days of His life on earth.

Plump, bustling, responsible Martha, a widow who had acted as both mother and father to her sister, Mary, and their brother, Lazarus, was bustling more than usual on a crisp, breezy evening in late winter. Lazarus had just returned from a day in Jerusalem, a short walk away from the quiet, peaceful little suburban village of Bethany, with the happy news that the Master would be there for dinner.

"The disciples with Him, Lazarus?" Martha was fairly sure His men would be there; after all, they had eaten her superior cooking at every opportunity for months now.

"They'll all be here, Martha, you know that!" Her gentle brother smiled, proud of her, even while he ducked inwardly, preparing for the sudden onslaught of busyness he knew would begin at once.

Martha's home was large and spacious, set well back in a grove of thick green trees, surrounded by the flower gardens Lazarus loved to tend. Until Jesus came into their lives, Martha's time hung heavily on her hands. She worked every minute at something, but beyond making a home for Mary and Lazarus, her life had little purpose.

Martha loved to talk, but she and Mary found it difficult to converse together, in spite of their devotion to each other. When Mary talked, she liked to think about what she was saying, and in order to think, she wanted to be walking quietly through the gardens or sitting down with no activity to distort her thoughts. Martha could talk without ceasing, but her activity also never ceased.

"To me, that's just idle chatter, not conversation," Mary always said, and Lazarus would laugh at them both and be thankful that he had two sisters who loved him as Mary and Martha loved their brother.

It was a normal, sometimes hectic, happy family, well respected all over Jerusalem, a family of prestige and good name.

"Do you think He's on His way here by now, Lazarus?"

"Should be here soon, Martha," her brother answered. "And He'll be tired tonight. They were cruel and vicious in town today. They stoned Him again."

Martha stopped bustling, her arms piled high with clean linens, her broad, kind face wrinkled with sorrow and concern. Martha loved Him.

"I know what you're thinking, sister, but He got away. He seems to be able to escape them almost miraculously. Even worse than the stones today, though, were their crude, constant jeers and questions and taunts. I don't know how He stands it! What He teaches is so amazing—so full of truth, so needed by everyone of those shallow, pigheaded people, it was all I could do to keep from throwing stones at *them!*"

Mary had slipped into the room where they stood talking. "Did they harm Him, Lazarus? Did they harm the Master today? Is He coming? Will I get to see Him tonight?"

"Yes, they're coming, Mary, and here I stand with all there is yet to do!" Martha flounced out of the room toward the kitchen off the back garden, and Mary and Lazarus were alone.

"He escaped them, Mary. They stoned Him again, or tried to. He's the most patient Man who ever lived on the earth. Nothing stops Him. It's like He's on a time schedule. There is so much He means to do, and nothing will stop Him."

"He loves them," Mary said simply. "He loves every single one of their ugly hearts!" Her troubled, sensitive face grew quiet. "And I love Him."

"I know you do," her brother said, touching her shoulder, "so do I."

"I think you're His favorite person, Lazarus, after His disciples."

"I know He loves me," the young man said, "but no more than anyone else. It's just that the Master *can* love everyone best."

As Mary and Lazarus stood talking about Him, Jesus and His men were walking steadily toward their home. They had crossed the valley from Jerusalem, climbed the Mount of Olives, and after what seemed a long, long time to Mary, but only a matter of minutes to busy Martha, they were there.

The ample stone house and its flowering gardens welcomed Him, and He welcomed the sight. He was tired, but this was home for now, and here He found His dear friends waiting for Him. He sat relaxed in the vine-cooled comfort of the front portico, with Lazarus, the disciples and Mary. The men talked a great deal about the day, their tensions lessening as the peace of the house of Bethany blurred the memory of the difficult hours among the hot crowds and the taunts and the flying stones. Now and then one of the men called jokingly after Martha as she appeared and disappeared within the house, directing the servants, working along with them making certain this would be a pertect meal.

It was not customary for a woman to sit talking with the men, but Mary followed her heart, not custom, and her heart remained as close to Him as possible through every minute of her life these days. In spite of His tiredness, He carefully repeated for Mary's eager ears much of what He had tried to teach at the Temple that day.

"I am the Good Shepherd," He said, "and I recognize My own. My own, in turn, recognize Me; just as the Father knows Me, and I know the Father—and I lay down My life for My sheep."

Mary's dark blue eyes were spilling tears, as she whispered, "I know You would lay down Your life for us."

"Mary! Mary!" Martha's big voice shattered the tender moment as she pounded out of the house and across the portico, wiping her pudgy hands on a linen towel.

"Lord," Martha complained comfortably, "don't you care that my sister is letting me do all the work alone? A dinner to see to for fourteen hungry men, and here she sits like a queen under the trees! Tell her to take hold with me!"

Jesus smiled at Martha, glad for her naturalness with Him. The men chuckled and waited to see how He would handle this little domestic situation.

Still smiling at her, He said, "Martha, Martha, you are anxious and bustling about many matters, when there is need of but few—or even of only one thing. Your sister, Mary, has selected the good portion. And she is not to be deprived of it!"

The tense moment passed. In a moment, good-hearted

Martha laughed at herself—a little anyway—and hurried back to the kitchen to finish preparing the dinner.

* * *

The Master was never superficial. He couldn't be; He was God Himself, in the flesh. And He knew both Mary and Martha better than they could ever have known themselves. Everyone knew how different they were, and He knew not only this, but the difference in the *spiritual places* where they each stood.

The superb hospitality He found in Martha's home was extremely important to Him. No one enjoyed her cooking more than He enjoyed it. No one found her spacious home more beautiful, more inviting. But always He had the real issues in full view. He could not be distracted from them, even by His tired body and His human need of Martha's services.

When He told the perspiring, hard-working older sister that her younger sister had made the wise choice, He was in no way belittling Martha, nor being ungrateful for her care. He was showing His deep love for her by going straight to the heart of the matter. He did not say that Mary should *not* be helping her sister; what He said was that if there is a choice, it is the better choice to show concern for the feeding of one's spirit than for the feeding of one's stomach. Perhaps Mary should have helped more. Obviously she was not the domestic type like her sister. But again, it seems plausible, since this incident is told in some detail in the Scriptures, that Jesus knew Martha to be too centered in her housework to the neglect of her soul. Being utterly realistic in all His discernments about all persons, He knew the *exact state* of Martha's inner self; most likely she was totally unconscious of this lopsidedness within her. This woman felt generous, and she was generous. She showed her genuine caring for Him and for her family in the only way she knew to show it—by handling everything with a vigor that sometimes tired them all just to watch!

We have all been in homes where the faithful woman of the house inadvertently makes us feel like burdens to her. It took a long time for me to realize that this was simply not true! I happen to dislike preparing dinner for anyone, including myself. I will always choose the simplest possible thing to prepare. Housework in all its aspects is a foreign

field to me. I do my share of it, but I don't like it. This has
nothing whatever to do with virtue or lack of it. Mary obviously enjoyed using her brain instead of her hands. This
also was neither right nor wrong. Mary and Martha *were*
as different as day and night, and Jesus accepted them that
way. But it so happened that in the final eternal analysis,
Mary's concentration upon what He had to say that night
was going to stand her in better stead. She would gain ultimately, and since He did love Martha as much as He
loved Mary, He wanted the best for Martha, too.

He did not scold Martha from annoyance on His part;
rather He was teaching her from love. He was quieting any
false guilt which Mary might have been carrying, too,
simply because she was so different from her practical
hard-working sister, whose accomplishments showed out-
wardly.

If possible, He wanted to give Martha a chance to see
for herself, that her ego was somewhat involved in those
splendid dinners she prepared. He appreciated the fact that
a woman like Martha could find fulfillment in domesticity;
this is as He planned it in the beginning. But fulfillment
and ego-padding differ greatly. That Martha's ego was
being padded was evident in the fact that she grew irritated
and complained in front of guests. We all grow weary of
well-doing now and then, but *if* we truly enjoy what we are
doing, however hard it may be, we seldom complain or
become annoyed. My back grows weary after several hours
at my typewriter, but writing so fulfills me and I enjoy it so
much, I even enjoy the aches and pains. Like you and
Martha, I do my complaining when for some reason I feel
stepped on. Jesus wants to clear up these points with us all.
And when they are cleared up, we like Mary, find that
quite naturally, we will begin to choose the better way.

Martha Ran to Meet Him — He Called for Mary

In January of the year A.D. 30, Jesus and His men
stopped coming to the home of Mary and Martha at Bethany. The violence broke against Him in Jerusalem with
such force that He and the disciples left for Perea, beyond
the Jordan River, and looped northward through Jericho
and Ephraim, preaching and healing all those who flocked
to Him.

Lying on some hillside for a night's rest, they must have
longed for the comfort and hospitality of Martha's home,

but as always, the Master's central longing was toward the people themselves.

Early in February, a message came from Martha and Mary, delivered to Him by a young boy who caught up with them at the weary end of a long, crowd-filled day.

"The one You love is ill," the message said, and He knew they were asking Him to come.

Without explaining why, Jesus waited two days before starting the journey back to Bethany. The disciples made use of every moment of the time, vainly trying to persuade Him not to go. They all knew His life was in danger in Jerusalem, and they all knew He was aware of it too. Still no one was surprised when He said finally, "Let us go back to Judea." They were surprised and puzzled, however, when He added, "Our friend, Lazarus, is asleep, but I am setting out to wake him up."

"But, Lord, if he is asleep, that probably means he will recover—that he has passed the crisis time."

"Lazarus is dead," He declared, "and for your sakes I am glad I was not present, so that you may believe. I will go to him now."

Back in Bethany, the beautiful home was filled with friends and relatives and the merely curious from Jerusalem and all the surrounding area. Lazarus was a well-known young man, respected by everyone who knew him even by reputation. The hired mourners were there weeping and wailing into their tear bottles, but had it not been the custom, they would not have needed professional mourners. His friends and family grieved deeply for the gentle young man who had died when his life seemed only to be beginning.

Hour after hour since they sent their message, Mary and Martha watched for some sight of Jesus. Their brother had grown weaker and then he had died. All through his funeral, the two sisters kept thinking Jesus would come; and now that Lazarus had been buried four days, they still watched for Him, as the mourning days continued in their home under the big shade trees, surrounded by the gardens Lazarus had loved and tended.

Over and over Martha wondered aloud where He could be. Those who had come to spy on Him for the authorities in Jerusalem, watched with her, taking in her every word. Mary withdrew more and more to herself in her grief. She said little, but like Martha, she still waited for Jesus.

Then someone told Martha that the Master was entering

the village with His men. Pushing through the throng of mourners and visitors, she ran heavily over her wide portico, across the flower-filled yard and down the lane toward Him. She was out of breath and talking rapidly when she reached Jesus' side.

"Lord, Lord, if You had been here, I know my brother would not have died! Why didn't You come? Why?"

He gave her a moment to steady herself. Her voice gentled. "And yet, even as I complain to You, Lord, now that I am face to face with You, I know that even yet, whatever You ask of God, He will grant You."

What she said to Him seemed almost a contradiction, but He knew exactly where Martha was in her spiritual pilgrimage. She did not confuse Him at all. He made no explanations about His late arrival, but merely said, "Martha, your brother will rise again."

For a moment there was hope in her swollen eyes; then she supposed He was merely trying to teach her. He was, but not the way Martha thought. And being Martha, always wanting to please, she tried to please Him then: "Yes, I know that he will rise again at the resurrection on the last day, but—"

"Martha, *I* am the Resurrection and the Life."

Martha stared at Him. So did His disciples, who had never heard Him express Himself that way before.

"I am the Resurrection and the Life; the believer in Me will live even when he dies, and everyone who lives and believes in Me shall never, never die. Do you believe this, Martha?"

"Yes, Lord, I have faith that You are the Christ, the Son of God, who was to come into the world."

He had led her from her moment of grieving confusion to her first clear statement of faith.

Martha seldom took time to let anything soak in, and she didn't take time now. Her suddenly light heart propelled her toward Mary, who sat alone in the house. "Mary, Mary! The Master has come and is asking for you."

Mary ran swfitly to Jesus and fell at His feet weeping.

He waited for her to speak first. "Lord, had You been here, my brother would not have died."

The same words Martha had spoken, but to Him they were not the same. He saw into each sister's heart; their words mattered little.

He did not try to teach Mary more, she already knew.

He merely wept with her. And after learning where
Lazarus was buried, He strode toward the tomb in the garden, a storm of grief tearing His body as He walked; His
spirit indignant at death itself for the grief and sorrow it
caused His loved ones! His weary being was suddenly
energized with a new desire to do battle with all that
caused death and suffering in His Father's world.

Standing near the entrance to the grave where Lazarus
had now lain four days, He said in a clear, firm voice:
"Remove the stone." When it was rolled aside, Jesus began
to talk quietly to His Father.

"Father, I thank You for having heard Me. I know You
always do hear Me; but on account of the people standing
here, I speak, so that they may believe that You have sent
Me."

He took a step back from the open grave, now mingling
its death and spice smells with the quick spring air, and
shouted: "Lazarus, come out!"

Mary and Martha stared with the others at the dark,
silent opening of the grave where they had laid the body of
their brother.

Some loose stones scraped the rock floor of the tomb.
Mary gasped and pressed her mouth with both her hands.
The people strained to see inside and then caught their
breath at the first sight of movement . . . white, dim, slow,
as Lazarus sat up, stood up, and hobbled out into the early
spring sun, bound hand and foot in the winding sheet, with
the burial napkin still tied around his face.

"Untie him," Jesus said exultantly. "Untie him, and give
him a chance to move!"

*   *   *

There are two deep truths for us here. Jesus did not expect Martha to know what she did not know. She spoke
the same words to Him which Mary spoke a few minutes
later, but they meant a totally different thing. Martha
loved Him with all she understood of Him. So did Mary.
But what they each understood was not the same. His
heart ached for Mary in her grief. It ached for Martha in
both her grief and her lack of light concerning Him. He
acted with them both according to what He *knew* about
them, not according to what they *said* to Him.

Gently, carefully, right there on the road, He brought
Martha to the point of seeing that He was the Son of God.

Mary already knew it. She had chosen the better part, by sitting hour after hour exposed to His words and His Person. Martha had been busy doing things for Him, with little time to listen to and absorb His teaching. What Martha did was a needed service and not to be minimized at all. But He was intent upon teaching them balance. Perhaps Mary should help out more around the house. Surely Martha should be less occupied with her busyness. Mary already knew, so He was free simply to *be* with her in her grief. He had to take time (and gladly) to teach Martha, but He could join Mary in her weeping.

At the open grave of their brother, balance probably came to them both. Here He demonstrated what His Father had planned to bring to completion in a few weeks for the whole world through Him. And as He brought their brother back to them with a word, He not only showed them His authority over death, He left a message for us which can bring the freedom of new life into all our human relationships.

Jesus said to them, "Untie him, and give him a chance to move!"

We pray, asking God for a multitude of things for our loved ones, and at the same time we ask, we are keeping them *tied* by some conscious or unconscious act or attitude of our own. Creative love pushes back the barriers; creative love unties the ropes; creative love gives its loved ones room to move!

Jesus raised Lazarus from the dead, but then He gave those standing about something specific to do: *they were to untie him and give him room to move about.*

We tie our loved ones by possessiveness, jealousy, lack of trust, by self-concern, by making decisions for them, by resentments. Jesus said we are to untie them, give them room to move about and then leave them to Him.

19. SALOME, MOTHER OF JAMES AND JOHN

A Woman Who Lost Her Confusion

The orderly, comfortable home of Salome, wife of Zebedee, was never again the same after the day her two sons, John and James, became disciples of Jesus. Most scholars agree that Salome, an intelligent, energetic woman, was the sister of Jesus' mother, Mary, but the circumstances of their married lives differed greatly. Mary's husband, Joseph, was never a well-to-do man, while Zebedee, the husband of Salome, owned a prosperous fleet of fishing boats, and their home on the shores of the Sea of Galilee at Capernaum was large and staffed with servants. Both her sons worked with their father, and until the day they met Jesus, took for granted the fact that they would follow Zebedee's profession.

Zebedee was a responsible husband, a good provider, but a man of violent temper, and when his sons decided to become disciples of this new Master from Nazareth, the old man grumbled and complained, but lost the family argument when Salome stood firmly with her sons.

"Just because this Master is your sister's son!"

"No, Zebedee, because I believe He is of God, and we dare not stand in the way of our sons' obedience to the Lord God."

Zebedee grumbled and went back to his boats, and the two young men, James and John, left their work to follow the One whom they believed was sent from God to deliver Israel from her bondage. They followed Him with their mother's full approval and support.

In fact, after her sons had been among His intimate circle of disciples for almost three years, toward the end of the earthly ministry of Jesus, Salome's encouragement turned to open ambition for her sons.

The pressure upon Jesus was now acute. He and His disciples were weary but determined to waste no valuable remaining time. His men understood little of His urgency, but they were loyal and worked with Him among the pushing, demanding multitudes who gathered wherever they went. A week before Passover, enroute south from Jericho toward the Holy City, they were joined on the road by throngs of pilgrims from Galilee once more making the annual journey to the Temple of God. In the crowd was Mary, the mother of Jesus, and her sister, Salome. The women were overjoyed at this unexpected meeting with their sons, and Salome and Mary talked about the change in James and John.

"They've always been high-strung, Mary—with tempers almost as quick as Zebedee's. But they have never been so depressed and worried as now. I'm going to talk with Jesus about my boys. I'll never rest until I know everything is going well for them. They both have a marvelous future with Him. I have stood behind them from the first against their father's wishes. I can't desert them now. After all, Mary, you know both boys did give up a great deal to follow Jesus!"

Mary looked after her sister with deep concern, not understanding just why, but feeling sure in her heart that somewhere Salome was missing the point.

James and John were not alone in their fear and worry over the future. After all, Jesus was going to Jerusalem. No one could stop Him now, and they all knew what could happen to Him there. For the third time He had taken them aside and said: "Take notice! We are going up to Jerusalem and the Son of Man shall be betrayed to the chief priests and the scribes; they will sentence Him to death and hand Him over to the Gentiles to be mocked and scourged and crucified, and on the third day He shall be raised."

He *must* be speaking in another kind of parable, they reasoned. This could not happen to their Master, and yet they feared His words were not parabolic.

In spite of their anxiety for Him, James and John agreed to go with their mother to speak to Jesus. "After all," she had reminded them, "Jesus is my nephew, and it's a mother's duty to see that her sons' way is smoothed if possible."

The three came to Jesus and kneeled before Him.

"What do you wish?" He asked of Salome.

"Jesus, say that these, my two sons, shall sit one at Your right and one at Your left, in Your kingdom."

He was not surprised at her ambitious request. He knew Salome. From the beginning He had appreciated her support of her sons in their work with Him, but He had not been confused as to her motive. Like everyone else, she believed He would set up an earthly kingdom for the people of Israel, with Himself as its king. He understood her reasoning. Salome wanted a reward in this kingdom for her sons who had left so much to follow Him.

"Salome," He said, "you do not know what you are asking." Then He turned to James and John. "Can you both drink the cup I am about to drink? More than you know now, you shall indeed drink my cup. But to sit at My right and My left is not Mine to grant! It is for those for whom it has been prepared by My Father."

Sorrowfully, Jesus turned to His other disciples, sensing their anger at this presumptuous request. "You know that the rulers of the Gentiles lord it over them, and their superiors oppress them. With you it is different: whoever among you wants to be great, must be your minister, and whoever wants to be first, shall be your servant! Just as the Son of Man did not come to be served, but to serve, and to give His life a ransom for many."

Not one among them, the women included, could remember one time when He had not been eager to serve them all. Salome said no more to Him about her sons. James and John said no more. He had given His life to them along every dusty, long mile of their way for almost three years. Now He was asking no more than to continue to give it.

When His time came, Salome was among those loyal women at His cross with Mary of Magdala, and His mother. She had believed in Him and supported Him with her means and her spirit. At the foot of His cross, she believed in Him with a changed heart, a heart opened to see that the greatest in His kingdom would always be the person with a servant's heart.

She stood at His cross serving the only way she knew, with her love. She was there at His empty tomb, finding her real reward, but forgetting her old need for it.

*   *   *

Salome was a good woman—faithful, loyal, energetic in

her service and her support of the earthly ministry of Jesus
of Nazareth. But it took His heartbreaking display of patience the day she attempted to secure the choice seats for
her sons to dispel her human ambition and clarify for her
the real meaning of love and greatness. He did not rebuke
her severely; He took time to teach her and the others
about authentic giving, which always leads to true
greatness.

This woman meant well. She had the interest of her sons
at heart, and she acted on it. A commendable thing,
humanly speaking. But in the shame of that moment on
the road to Jerusalem, she became a new woman, with a
new and true sense of responsibility. He showed her and
she *saw* that she could serve both her sons and Him in a
deeper way. We know she saw this, because every other
mention of her in the gospel accounts is of quiet, submissive service to Him in His terrible need.

It was perfectly natural for Salome to want her sons to
get ahead, but it was also perfectly natural for her to put
her emphasis in the wrong place. Until He spoke to her as
He did, on the eve of His own suffering, she simply did not
see greatness in its true perspective. The world's concept of
greatness is the exact reverse of God's concept of it.

Mothers today who push their children into places of
prominence, miss the point as surely as Salome missed it,
and with far less excuse than she had. She made her attempt to gain seats of honor for her sons *before* she
watched Him pour out His life on the cross of Calvary,
before she saw true greatness spring from His giving as she
stood in wonder and awe with His mother and the other
Mary before His empty tomb. We can know the marks of
greatness in retrospect now, and so we have no excuse to
seek it in false positions.

There is no indication that Salome ever pushed her boys
again after that day. She had given them to Him, but she
still held the strings, until her own heart began to glimpse
the characteristics of greatness in the poured-out life.

20. CLAUDIA PROCULA

A Woman Who Lacked Influence

Claudia Procula, the wife of Pilate, the Roman Governor of Judea, lived for most of the year at the governor's luxurious palace to the north of Caesarea Philippi on the sea. Each year, however, she came with Pilate to Jerusalem where he would be needed to see that order prevailed among the thousands of Jews who streamed into the Holy City for the Feast of the Passover. In Jerusalem, Claudia and Pilate stayed at the lavishly furnished Herodian Palace, and lying on her wide, silk-covered bed on the night before the Feast Day, Claudia had a dream.

There was unusual confusion in the dark streets of the Holy City that night, confusion that tore at her very soul, but about which she could tell no one. Certainly not Pilate. The last two trips to Jerusalem had been strangely meaningful for Claudia, and this year she had come with a deep sense of urgency to get there—perhaps actually to see Him again. The wide windows of the Herodian Palace opened out above the crowded city, and once two years ago, she had seen Him healing a lame man, and last year she had seen Him twice, talking earnestly to a crowd and then stopping on one of the narrow, cluttered streets to help an old beggar to his feet. Who was this Man? Claudia questioned her servants, and bit by bit she learned that He was an itinerant preacher from Galilee, who spoke as no other man had ever spoken, and who never grew too weary to be of the smallest service to the most insignificant man or woman.

Through the years between those visits to Jerusalem, Claudia had thought about Him often, and with every thought, her heart seemed to open—toward what she did not know.

Now she was back in Jerusalem, and from the servants she had learned that His life was in danger. Those troublesome priests at the Jewish Temple wanted Him out of the way, but because of their stupid laws about not killing a man, they were attempting to trick her husband, Pilate, into taking the action himself.

Claudia slept little that night, her thoughts disturbed and tormented by His trouble. She had never spoken to Him, but she buried her eyes in her pillows attempting to shut out even her thoughts of what might be happening to Him as they jerked Him with ropes through the ancient streets from before her husband, sitting pompously on the Judgment Seat on the balcony of the Tower of Antonia, to that half-drunken Herod and back again. Claudia had heard, at least, of the God of Israel, and her heart cried to Him to help this good Man, Jesus. Then she sat up laughing at herself. How would the God of those wicked priests help a good Man like the Master? And yet, Jesus of Nazareth was a Jew also. Her thoughts careened and twisted from half-uttered prayers to a God whose name she did not know, to self-accusation for allowing her sleep to be interrupted by a mere uprising among the people of the streets! At last she slept a little, just long enough to dream the dream that brought her out of her bed, only half awake, but driven to do something to stop the injustice she now knew was about to take place.

Quickly she penned a note to Pilate and dispatched it at once to be delivered to him personally as he sat on the Seat of Judgment before the howling mob. Claudia threw open her window that faced the Tower of Antonia. She could see the torch lights, ugly and red against the night sky. The shouts of the angry mob came and went, and during the lulls, she supposed Pilate was speaking to them. *Hurry!* her thoughts urged the messenger on his way through the crowded streets. *Hurry! Oh, please hurry before it is too late!*

On his Judgment Seat above the crowd, Pilate sat uneasily; the Man Jesus, swaying and injured, stood beside him. Desperately, Pilate shouted to the crowd: "Whom shall I release to you—Barabbas or Jesus, who is called the Christ?"

Their answer shocked him.

"Barabbas! Release Barabbas to us!"

Pilate slumped in his ornate chair, debating uncertainly what he would do next. An attendant handed him a note in his wife's own handwriting. He unfolded it quickly, irritated with Claudia for bothering him at a moment like this. The note read: "Do nothing, I beg you, to that innocent Man, for I was deeply affected this morning while dreaming about Him!"

For an instant Pilate longed to pay attention to his wife. Caught as he was between the howling mob backed by the priests of the Temple, and his own ambition toward Rome to keep order at any cost, he would have grabbed at an easy way out. Instead he crumpled the note: "What does my foolish wife know of such things?" Jumping suddenly to his feet, as annoyed with his own helplessness as with the mob and Claudia, he shouted, for want of anything new to say: "What shall I do then, with Jesus who is called the Christ?"

"Crucify Him! Crucify Him! Let Him be crucified!"

In the end, Pilate gave in to the angered crowd, but before he ordered the crucifixion, he washed his hands of the deed before the people themselves, crying, "I am innocent of this good Man's blood. It is your concern!"

Claudia's note had disturbed him, but not enough to stir Pilate to sufficient courage against the people of Jerusalem.

*   *   *

There are those who believe Claudia may have been a secret believer in Jesus. Perhaps she was. Certainly she had been convinced in her heart that He was a good Man, not worthy of execution, harming no one, only blessing all those who came in contact with Him.

Claudia did a courageous and daring thing, sending her plea for His life to Pilate in that tense moment. But, her good act was weakened because, if she was a believer, she had kept it such a secret, her plea lacked influence with her husband.

Evidently Pilate had never heard anything definite about Jesus until that night. The whole incident was new and troublesome and difficult for him. Had Claudia begun sharing her feelings about this Man before that night, she might have prevailed upon her husband. But she had not, and her note came only as an annoying surprise, for which he was not prepared.

Our defense of Christianity today can be weakened in exactly the same way, if we keep our faith a secret. When, in some sudden emergency, we reveal it to those who have heard little of Him, how can we expect them to listen to us?

How can we expect them not to be annoyed, not to turn away, ignoring our urgency? For that matter, if we have not openly pursued our walk with Christ, how can we expect our own inner strength to be great enough for the times of sudden tension and tragedy? Claudia made a last desperate effort to defend Him, but her influence was not great enough. Her interest in this Man was all news to her husband, and being Pilate, he could not have been expected to pay much attention to this last minute effort on the part of his well-meaning but ineffectual wife.

21. MARY OF MAGDALA

A Woman Whose Mind Was Healed

Near the place where He fed the four thousand, Jesus entered the town of Magdala, on the northwest shore of the Sea of Galilee. He had come here to rest, but as always, when he walked toward a town, word spread that He was coming, and from the houses and shops those who were well, dragged and led and pushed their friends and relatives with blind eyes and crippled legs and demented minds.

In the gathering crowd shoving toward Him that day at the edge of Magdala, was a tall young woman in her late twenties, her disheveled hair not quite hiding what could have been a beautiful face, her thin shoulders hunched with fear. A relative dragged her forward, as she dragged back, cursing and then weeping, her dark eyes struggling to focus first on some perspiring face nearby and then on the ground. "This way, Mary, this way!" Her relative jerked her arm and she jerked back. "He's right over there!"

When she saw Him, her curses stopped abruptly and she screamed. Jesus turned to her, and the young woman screamed again, stunning the crowd to near silence.

Her relative dropped the possessed woman's hand and stepped back anxiously. Mary of Magdala took one faltering step toward the Master, flung herself on the ground at His feet, and wept violently. Slowly He walked to her, bent down and touched her shoulder. She screamed again, turning her tortured young face directly up to Him, her eyes wild and circled with deep shadows, her mouth opening and closing. But no words came and she wept again, burying her head in the dust where He stood.

"She is possessed by a devil," her relative ventured, addressing Jesus, "at least seven devils!"

He touched her again and waited. The crowd waited, too, silent now. Then Mary raised her head slowly, her mouth closed and quiet. One hand smoothed her tousled

165

hair, and she looked about her, surprised to find herself there, as though she remembered none of the dragging and the screaming and the pushing through the crowd. Mary was standing up now, facing this Man from Nazareth, a calm composure filling her eyes, tension lines falling from her young face.

He smiled at her reassuringly and she smiled faintly too, for a moment still standing there, testing her new freedom, not daring to move. Then her shoulders straightened, her head lifted, and as the crowd watched in shock and wonder, Mary of Magdala, in full command of both her mind and her heart, fell to her knees before Him, to begin a singular kind of total worship that lasted for all the rest of her life on earth.

*   *   *

Most of us think of Mary of Magdala as a redeemed harlot. There is little or no reason for this, although she has been associated in the minds of many with the woman who broke her alabaster box of ointment and poured it on Jesus' feet. So widespread is this, to me, erroneous concept of Mary of Magdala, that the word *Magdalene* has come to be synonymous with a redeemed prostitute. Be that as it may, we are specifically told in the Bible that Mary of Magdala possessed seven demons and that Jesus cast them all out.

Whether or not we associate demon possession with our twentieth century concept of mental disease is also rather beside the point here. This Mary may have been a woman of questionable morals, too, but she was also *not* in command of her mind. The fact that He had to "cast out seven devils" would seem to indicate a rather severe mental sickness. There is no factual basis for our description of how she met Jesus, but the important thing for us here is to realize that she was in need of mental healing and she got it!

It is unlikely that any other single deviation causes more torment in human relationships than when a person is psychopathic, or even obviously neurotic. Although we have told her story as one having a severe psychopathic affliction, extremely neurotic women (and men) can cause just as much trouble and confusion. These are the persons around whom we tread softly, for fear of setting off another explosion. To reason with them is futile; they simply do not have the ability to follow reasoning. To shout and scold is just as futile; they can usually shout louder and their ability to use their tongues as whiplashes against us surpasses our scolding. We stand utterly helpless to control or to help them.

I believe God heals through many means, the new drugs and psycotherapy, as well as by direct intervention in prayer; often by a combination of all three. The only point I want to make here is that Mary's relative did the only thing anyone can do: she took the afflicted person to Someone who could help. It is a common folly among Christians to crash in where an intelligent angel would fear to tread! I have been guilty of this in the past, but never again. Those of us not trained to understand the human mind should not try to urge our thinking on someone with even a trace of mental sickness. Only a competent psychiatrist can do this. But we can pray, and we can pray with faith, remembering the new, lasting poise which came to Mary of Magdala when Jesus touched her.

He Could Trust Mary to See Him First

With His mother and her sister, Salome, Mary of Magdala stood at His cross with Him, quiet and steady in the midst of her anguish and grief. No one there loved Him more than she; He had done so much for her. When they laid Him in the tomb of Joseph of Arimathea, Mary was there, too, and before dawn on Sunday, the first day of the new week, she hurried through the still silent streets of Jerusalem with His mother and Salome, toward His grave. Under one arm, Mary carried a bundle of aromatic spices and a box containing vials of oil and rose water; with the other arm, she helped Salome support His mother. The women were going to finish caring for His dear, broken body, now that the Sabbath was over.

The path to the tomb in the garden was narrow; here they had to walk single file. Mary Magdalene went first, to hold back the low hanging tree boughs laden with blossoms, to watch for rough places on the path, to kick stones from His sorrowing mother's way, to face first the stern Roman guard stationed there to see that His disciples did not steal His body.

"Will they allow us to go inside His tomb?" Salome grew nervous as they neared the place where they had laid Him.

"We will face that in due time," Mary Magdalene said firmly. "They cannot object to our caring for His body. Let them watch us, if they must!" They picked their way, down the gentle slope that led to the mouth of the tomb, Mary Magdalene out in front a few steps, her lovely face quiet with resolve.

Because she was leading the way, she saw it first!

Hurrying along behind His mother, Salome wailed, "Who will roll away the stone for us?"

"No one," Mary Magdalene said quietly. "No one needs to roll it away."

The stone was off to one side, and the grave stood open, smellng of the spices and ointments with which Nicodemus and Joseph had hurriedly rubbed His body the day He died. The three women threw back their heavy veils. Salome cried out. His mother leaned heavily for a moment against an olive tree, and then bent forward, as Mary stooped to peer inside the dark tomb. When she ventured inside, the other two women followed her, and there, to their right, sat a young man dressed in pure white. Salome cried out again in fright.

"Do not be terrified!" The young man's voice was quiet and reassuring. "You are looking for Jesus of Nazareth, who was crucified."

Mary Magdalene nodded, too overwhelmed to speak.

"He is risen! He is not here—see the place where they laid Him! Go now, tell His disciples—and Peter—that He precedes you into Galilee."

"Galilee?" His mother whispered. "He has gone home?"

"Yes, there you will see Him, just as He told you."

Then the young man was gone. The women hurried outside, their eyes wide, their hearts pounding. Dawn was coming now to the sky, and all the birds were awake suddenly, like their hope.

"Go to your room to rest," Mary urged His mother. "I will go alone to tell Peter and John."

His two beloved disciples ran back to the tomb with her, grumbling all the way, suspecting Mary's old trouble had returned, that she had merely imagined such a thing as an empty tomb.

When they saw it for themselves, they believed her, but went their way again, leaving her alone in the garden. She was glad to be there; her grief ran deeper than most people realized. Now she could weep as much as she needed to weep, and no one would think her mad again. For His sake, because He had healed her mind, she had controlled herself. Now, standing alone in the spring sunlight slanting down through the tall cedar trees, she could weep freely.

Her grief had lifted somewhat at the sight of the empty tomb and the presence of the Angel of the Lord, but now that she was alone, the weight rolled back on her heart. Was she to be deprived of even that last chance to show Him her love, her gratitude for all He had done for her? Was He gone now forever? Even His body?

She wept bitterly for several minutes, like a lost child. Then she wanted to go inside His tomb again, to be near the stones that had known the dear weight of His body. There inside the tomb, one sitting at the head and one at the foot of the place where He had lain, were two angels in white robes. Together, as one sweet sounding voice, they said to her: "Woman, why are you crying?"

"Because they have taken away my Lord and I do not know what they have done with Him!"

Suddenly Mary could stand the stuffy tomb no longer. She turned and ran outside, breathing the clear, sweet air deeply, hating the thought of the blood and spice-encrusted tomb. Now she wanted to see Him alive; her desire to care for His dead body was suddenly forgotten.

In the garden outside the tomb, Mary was no longer alone. Someone else was there. She whirled around and heard the same question the two angels had asked her a moment before. "Woman, why are you crying? Whom do you seek?"

Was she sick in her mind again? Imagining this?

It must be the gardener, she reasoned. But it *was* a man; she was not mad, and she did need help.

"Sir, if you've carried Him away, tell me where you have put Him, and I'll take Him!"

"Mary!" Jesus' voice spoke her name tenderly.

Throwing back her veil, she looked full in His face. It was He. "Master! My Master!"

He was alive! Walking the earth again, with His goodness and gentleness and love. Her Saviour was not dead! Mary dropped to her knees and reached for His hand to kiss it and to bathe it with tears of joy.

"Do not cling to Me, Mary," He said patiently, "for I have not yet ascended to My Father."

She accepted this, not understanding, but obeying Him; not touching Him further. He was there. She could see His face and she could hear His voice. For now, for her, that was enough.

"Go now, Mary," He said, "to my brothers and tell them that I said, I ascend to My Father and your Father, to My God and your God."

Mary went swiftly, to do as He had asked. Her heart sang with joy as she ran. He had come to her *first*, calling her name! Not, she knew, because He loved her more, but because she was still there looking for Him, unable to give Him up.

*   *   *

If the disciples did not trust Mary's story about the open, empty tomb, remembering her old ways before He healed her, *He* trusted her. Her Master trusted her with the shock and the joy of the incredible moment through which she had just passed. He trusted her with seeing Him first because He knew the depths of her love and her need to see Him. He also trusted her mind with the shock of that moment because He had healed her mind and knew it was a complete healing.

Mary understood little at that bright, deep moment when she recognized Him as her risen Lord. She still had to learn that He had not come back merely as Lazarus had returned from the dead. She still did not know that He commanded her not to touch Him for a reason, that she would have to give Him up to go back to His Father, so the time could come when His Spirit would return to be with her forever. He did not give Mary special spiritual insight beyond the others when He healed her mind back in Magdala that day before the amazed throng of people who had known her madness for so long. He gave her no special discernment, but He did give her back a normal mind, and its normalcy and balance held through His crucifixion and His death, and now, with joy as great as her sorrow had been, her mind still held.

He did not appear to her first to test her sanity or mental balance after the healing, He came to her because He knew her mind and the unmixed motives of her obedient heart. He came to her also, without a doubt, because she was the one who was still there, needing some last sign of Him.

God, with all His giving heart, *can* only give us Himself as we recognize the depth of the need in our own lives.

22. DORCAS (TABITHA)

A Woman Who Practiced Her Faith

After Pentecost, the followers of Jesus went out with great energy and enthusiasm, not only to reach those who did not yet believe in Him, but to act on what they themselves believed. For a period, after His Spirit returned to them on the Jewish Feast of Pentecost, their love ran so high they were able to share equally even of their material possessions. The women were now an active part of the crusade of love, and it was the common thing for both women and men to give, not only of their money and property, but of their time and their energies to those less fortunate.

In this rarefied atmosphere of faith in action, it is all the more amazing when one woman was singled out as being extremely generous in her active faith. Dorcas, who lived in a good mud-brick house in the Mediterranean seaport city of Joppa, about thirty-four miles northwest of Jerusalem, was loved and leaned on by everyone who knew her. Even in the midst of such active Christianity, Dorcas' life was unusual in its selflessness. Most likely a woman of some means, she did not settle for giving only her money to further the cause of the Lord they all loved. Dorcas gave of herself.

Joppa, like all coastal towns, had great numbers of poor citizens. Many of them earned their living from the sea, and the wild Mediterranean winter storms wrecked their wooden boats, and often cast the men and the wreckage of their crafts back onto the shores of Joppa. The widows and children of the fishermen touched Dorcas' heart, but she did not stop with sympathy or mere alms. She spent hours in the upper room of her house by the sea, cutting and sewing undergarments and coats for those who otherwise would be clothed in rags. Her giving did not stop with the merely destitute; Dorcas' generosity of spirit included those in the thriving Christian circle in Joppa, too. The people all loved her, not only for her kindness, but for her contagious, bubbling personality.

171

"She always has a happy word for everyone," they said of her. "What would we ever do if anything happened to Dorcas?"

And then, one day, as she was busily sewing in her upper room, Dorcas' faithful heart failed, and she died suddenly. When her friends found her, their grief was uncontrollable. "No one can take her place," they moaned. "The rest of us can sew and make clothing for the poor, but no one is like Dorcas!"

Lovingly, the women washed her frail body and carried her to the same upper room where she had spent so many hours sewing garment after garment, and laid her on her couch there, all of them weeping.

Then someone remembered that Peter was preaching not ten miles away at Lydda, and a few had faith enough to believe that the big man of God could raise her from the dead. All of them wanted him to come anyway, to pray for them in their sorrow.

When Peter arrived a few days later on foot, with the two men from Joppa who had been sent to get him, he went straight to the upper room where Dorcas lay, surrounded by weeping widows and friends.

"Look," they exclaimed to Peter, "look at the rows of coats she has made—here are three half-finished. These bundles are all new undergarments made with her own hands for the poor who would otherwise live in rags. She not only clothed their bodies, Peter, she clothed their spirits with new hope."

Peter took in the situation in silence, then asked them all to leave him alone with Dorcas' body. On his knees in her sewing room, Peter prayed to the Lord God for guidance and faith. Then he turned to Dorcas' quiet form and cried, using the familiar Aramaic form of her name: "Tabitha, arise!"

Slowly she opened her eyes. When she recognized Peter, she smiled and sat up. Joyfully she grasped Peter's big hand and he pulled her to her feet. When he called the others back into the room, their shouts of gladness and thanksgiving to God were louder than their weeping had been a few moments before.

Dorcas was back with them again, to cheer them and to demonstrate for them all the rest of her life, the essence of a truly giving heart.

"This became known all over Joppa and many believed in the Lord."

*   *   *

God honored Peter's prayer for many reasons, we can be sure. We know how Jesus hated the sorrow left always in the wake of the death of a loved one. God also needed Dorcas alive and working for Him among the needy people whom He loved. But the Bible tells us that when it became known in Joppa, the big result was this: ". . . many believed in the Lord."

In attempting to draw some conclusions other than the superficial ones from this arresting little story of a woman who knew how to *give,* we need to be utterly realistic. There have been many, many other women who have worked as hard with a needle and a pair of scissors as Dorcas worked, who have given as unselfishly and as cheerfully of their time and energies, of themselves. Those left behind when these women died, grieved for them as Dorcas' friends grieved for her. We have no record that God raised any of these later women from the dead. Does this mean that Dorcas was special? Does it mean that there were more poorly clothed people in Joppa who needed her? Was she raised from the dead because the spiritual climate among those early Christians was so high? Perhaps. But most important here, as I see it, is that we do not need to hunt for a reason when God acts!

The Bible makes a particular point of mentioning that many people believed as a result of her resurrection. For the time and place, with limited methods of communication, this is certainly one reason God raised Tabitha from the dead. But here the facts must be examined. There has resulted from the New Testament story of this one woman's life, more world-wide service of the kind she gave, than Dorcas' swift fingers at their best could have managed. The Dorcas Society is world-wide and, because of it, millions upon millions of needy persons have been clothed and cared for.

Whatever His reasons for answering Peter's prayer, they are right reasons and they are God's reasons and we can let the matter rest. The insight for us is this: whether or not the result of a prayer of faith is spectacular as in the case of Dorcas, God does answer the prayer of faith and many are given a chance to become believers.

This entire episode is so authentically Christian, it seems inevitable that its results would have been anything but creative. Dorcas was a woman with a giving heart, with a life entirely dedicated to the will of God. The friends and neighbors who loved her stayed keenly aware of the still recent Resurrection of Jesus Christ. The new power which came at Pentecost was still fresh in their daily lives. God was mainly in control, therefore the entire incident had to be authentically Christian.

Is this power, this childlike faith impossible to us? Not unless the Spirit Himself has changed, has lessened Himself with the years. Of course, He has not. We have allowed the fog of busyness and mixed motives and spiritual procrastination to rise between His power and our lives.

It is we who are stale, and therefore amazed at this story. He is as fresh and willing as ever.

23. LYDIA

A Christian Professional Woman

Lydia almost always dressed in purple. It became her, but it was also good business. She was a seller of purple dye, the almost magical secretion that ran clear and white through the veins of a certain mollusk (shell fish), but which, when exposed to the sun, turned suddenly from deep purple to crimson, and made a permanent, strong dye for fabrics. Knowledge of dye-making was traditional in Lydia's family, and so closely had she remained in contact with her heritage that she had been named for Lydia, the region where her ancestors lived in Asia Minor. The Lydian purple market had flourished throughout the Graeco-Roman world, and Lydia's family undoubtedly were members of the renowned Dyers' Guild at Thyatira, where she was born.

As a successful business woman, Lydia left her home in Thyatira when her husband died, and moved to Philippi in Macedonia (Europe). Here she was greatly respected and loved by her friends and business associates. In spite of her professional success and popularity, however, this woman, Lydia, must have been sensitively aware of a lack in her personal life. She was a Gentile, but in A.D. 50, she had become a part of a small group of Jewish women who met together to worship the God of Abraham, and Lydia came to believe in Him as the true God.

Her home was large and comfortable, but perhaps because members of her Gentile family objected, or because Lydia herself still felt some hesitancy about being publicly associated with those who worshiped the true God, the little group met outside the gates of Philippi on the shady banks of the Gangites River, to study the ancient Scriptures and to pray to the Lord God.

They had never heard of Jesus Christ, but God heard their prayers for more light and spiritual encouragement, because Paul, then in Troas, had a vision in which he felt called to go into Macedonia with the Gospel of Christ.

175

Luke sailed with him, and they went by way of the island of Samothrace and Neapolis straight to Philippi where Lydia lived. Learning of this group of devout women who met on the banks of the river outside the city, Paul, Luke and Silas went there directly and found the women eager and open to the message of the risen Lord. Their hearts were well prepared to believe, and with great joy, Lydia and most of her group of Jewish friends welcomed the news that the Messiah had come.

If she had been somewhat embarrassed to meet in her own home with her Jewish friends, her new life in Christ put an immediate end to this mark of self-consciousness. Paul baptized them immediately in the little river, and Lydia insisted that Paul and his friends come to her large, spacious house in the city. This already attractive, intelligent, courageous woman who handled her own prosperous business in an era when women just did not do this, was filled with the new radiant boldness that characterized everyone in the early Christian church. Her home became the meeting place of a growing group of followers of the risen Lord, and Paul taught them and prayed with them there regularly.

One day when Paul and Silas were on their way to Lydia's home for a prayer meeting, Paul cast out the demon of clairvoyance from a young girl, whose occult powers had been a good source of income for a group of Philippian men. The men became so angered that they had Paul and Silas arrested, flogged and thrown into jail for causing a public disturbance. As the two followers prayed and praised the Lord in prison, an earthquake brought about not only their release, but the conversion of the jailer and his family; and as soon as Paul and Silas were outside, they went straight to Lydia's house to rejoice with the other Christians gathered there in prayer for their safety. A big group rejoiced greatly that night because now their number had grown to include many husbands and sons and brothers.

Lydia continued her business activities, but the center of her life was the indwelling Presence of the same Lord who had filled the lives of those who waited with His mother and His brothers that day in the upper room in Jerusalem.

*   *   *

It is important to realize that Lydia was not a down and

outer. She was a highly successful, cultivated professional
woman, with prestige and power in the city of Philippi. She
seemed to have everything, but she was perceptive enough
to face her inner emptiness and to take definite steps to try
to fill it with the true God.

I have long believed that God will move heaven and
earth to reveal Himself as He really is in Jesus Christ,
wherever He finds an open, seeking heart. Lydia and her
Jewish friends believed in the Lord God, and this same
Lord God sent Paul and Luke to bring them into full life
in Christ. Too many Christians now, miss the great point
of God, when they condemn and steer clear of the members of certain religious groups whose light is dim and incomplete. In most instances, these so-called apostate
groups are sincere, seeking human beings who are simply
in darkness about the reality of Jesus Christ. They have
heard words about Him in the twentieth century. It is almost impossible not to hear about Him with our plethora
of modern communications, but as true followers of the
God of patience and understanding and insight, dare we
believe that these people have really been exposed to Jesus
as He is? History could be changed if the hearts and attitudes of God's people could be changed toward the members of the cults and fringe groups. They are praying, as
Lydia and her friends prayed, and many are praying with
searching hearts. Even if we believe them to be praying
amiss according to *our* light, God is still able to move
heaven and earth for them as He did for Lydia and her
friends on the banks of the little river outside of Philippi.

Do you for one minute think Lydia and her friends
knew enough to pray that God would send two Christian
disciples to show them the way to Jesus Christ as their personal Saviour? They had never heard of Jesus Christ!
Their hearts were open when they prayed, however, and
this is what God looks for.

Instead of shunning, we can begin to pray for a Paul
and a Luke to be sent to the groups we shun. We can begin
to pray that God may give us a chance to be a Paul or a
Luke to them.

It is also interesting to me that even though Lydia
became fully centered in her new Christian life, she apparently did not become eccentric. She went on being Lydia, caring for her business, but sharing her home and her
energies with God. There is no record that she leaped off
dramatically after Paul when he left Philippi, bent on

becoming a great worker for Christ. She served Him where she was, in her old business, living her new life fully, in the presence of her customers and her business associates. She gave God a chance to get into the market place with her, and to reach hearts He may never have been able to reach, had Lydia begun to hunt for speaking dates and new mission fields. She lived Christ in Philippi, going about her business as usual; and around her there grew the caliber of Christian church to which Paul could write with such deep affection: "Every time I think of you, I thank my God." Paul's letter to the Philippians has been called "God's love letter." Paul was a human being, after all, and a rather opinionated one. He did not have natural affection for difficult, ego-centric people. He cared for them in Christ, and poured out his life attempting to help them grow up and mature in their new faith, but he evidently found Lydia and her friends balanced, open, easy to love. "It is quite appropriate for me to have you all in mind this way," he wrote to them, "because I have you in my heart, as all of you share with me in divine grace, whether it be in my imprisonment or in the defense and confirmation of the Gospel. For God is my witness how I yearn for you all with the deep-felt affection of Christ Jesus."

Lydia was not a down-and-outer, she was merely an incomplete woman, as all women are incomplete without Christ. Once she belonged to Him, Paul and everyone else found her easy to know and to love.

24. PRISCILLA

A Woman Who Dared to Use Her Mind

About six months after Paul left Lydia and her friends in the new church at Philippi, he entered into another deep friendship which sustained him through many difficulties with the new churches at both Ephesus and Corinth.

Paul had much in common with Priscilla, a Jewess from Rome, and her husband, Aquila, both converts to Jesus Christ. Like Paul, both Priscilla and Aquila were skilled tent makers, and he not only founded the church at Corinth in their home, he lived there, working side by side with them at his practical trade. Hour after hour, Paul sat with his two friends, as they wove goat's hair into narrow strips of dark brown or black cloth, to be sewn together into tents. With Priscilla especially, Paul carried on stimulating discussions of the deep things of God, as their handmade wooden looms slipped the coarse thread back and forth, back and forth. Priscilla sewed deftly and fast, and her quick mind probed Paul's fine store of knowledge of the Scriptures and the nature of God in Jesus Christ. She was no superficial church worker—this woman was a scholar—but she studied and learned with a humility as profound as her intellect.

During Paul's stay with them, he seemed to reach new intensity in his urgency to convince both Jew and Gentile that Jesus was the Christ. He spoke regularly in the synagogue, in spite of a continuous stream of abuse and opposition, and by the time Silas and Timothy joined him in Corinth, Paul was "possessed utterly by his message." The more the Jews opposed him, the more he longed to make contact with them, and after awhile, he moved from Priscilla's house to the house of another convert, Titus Justus, who lived next door to the synagogue. The aging Paul still visited Priscilla and Aquila often in their home, and they backed him up all the way with their prayers in behalf of the Jews.

179

One day, Paul came to tell them with great joy that Crispus, the leader of the synagogue, and his entire family now believed in Jesus Christ as the Messiah.

"God Himself has spoken to me concerning the abuse and the opposition I have endured," Paul told them as they ate together at Priscilla's house that day. "In a night vision—only last night," Paul went on, "the Lord said to me: 'Have no fear; but speak and do not keep still, because I am with you and none shall assault you to your hurt; because I have much people in this city.' "

Priscilla was a beloved leader of God's "much people" in Corinth, and she rejoiced when Paul decided to settle down there for an indefinite period of work in the Corinth church.

He stayed a year and a half, and when he sailed for Ephesus, Priscilla and Aquila sailed with him. Then in the late summer of A.D. 53, Paul left his two friends in charge of the church at Ephesus, although they begged him to stay, and moved on to Caesarea, Antioch, Galatia and Phrygia, teaching and strengthening the new churches all along his way.

Back in Ephesus, Priscilla and her husband were busy as always, weaving their tent cloth and greeting and teaching the Christians who made their house once more their meeting place. They were honored one night, when a brilliant and educated young man named Apollos, a native of Alexandria, attended one of their meetings. He was extremely popular as a speaker and taught with a burning passion all he knew about Jesus. Apollos not only spoke to their Christian church he taught with as much zeal in the synagogue.

Both Priscilla and Aquila liked the young man, and after talking it over with each other and with God, they invited him to their house alone for a private conversation. Apollos had his facts straight concerning the identity of the Man from Galilee, the necessity for repentance, faith and water baptism, but here his knowledge ended abruptly. Apollos had not had an opportunity, apparently, to learn the deeper truth of the indwelling Holy Spirit—the very moving force of the true Christian Church. His knowledge stopped with the teaching of John the Baptist.

Tenderly, carefully, Priscilla began to talk to him concerning the Holy Spirit who lived in the followers of Christ. With Aquila, she witnessed to His power in their own lives, in the lives of other Christians.

Apollos saw the truth at once, and from this brief encounter with these two Spirit-filled people, the brilliant, convincing young man went on to teach the full impact of the whole truth about Jesus Christ. Up to that time, Apollos had been drawing people to himself without realizing it. Once Priscilla and Aquila "explained the way of God more accurately to him," he drew his audiences *through* himself to Jesus Christ.

Paul loved his two friends to the end of his earthly life, mentioning them often in his letters. Just before he was beheaded by Nero in Rome, he sent his greeting to Prisca, showing his deep and affectionate love and respect for his dear sister in Christ, by using her familiar name.

After the death of Claudius, who had expelled the Jews from Rome, Priscilla and Aquila went back home to their native Italy. Her name can still be found on monuments in Rome to this day. Tertullias spoke of her as "the holy Prisca, who preached the gospel." *The Coemeterium Priscilla,* one of the oldest catacombs in Rome, was named for her. On the Aventine in Rome, a church bears her name—*Titulus St. Prisca.*

Since men always held the honored place in society during Priscilla's time, it is unique that in the Bible, her name is usually mentioned before her husband's name. Yet, this was no domineering woman. Priscilla, Paul's dear friend, was God's dear friend also. She dared to use her good mind, but she used it in total submission to the Lord God who held the central place in her creative and fruitful life.

* * *

Here is a woman about whom all women should think deeply. In a period when women were not encouraged to use their minds, she was not afraid to use hers. But there is no indication whatever that she ever misused it by either conceit or domination. Priscilla let the mind of Christ be in her, as her good friend Paul urged her to do. Her faith was expressed in no superficial doctrinal clichés. When she taught the Gospel of Christ, she lived it at the very moment the words poured from her lips. She slammed no doors in anyone's face because she "had it all straight."

Paul could trust Priscilla. She and her husband begged Paul to stay with them when they moved to Ephesus, but Paul knew by then, that this was no longer necessary. Her clarity of mind and purpose set him free to continue giving himself to other needy churches in other cities scattered over the known world. The Christians at Ephesus would be in good hands with Priscilla and Aquila.

Paul was known to become irritated and disturbed by some of his helpers. Never by Priscilla. He must have loved her deeply as his Christian sister. A woman in Paul's time was more likely to be a liability, but Priscilla, with her excellent mind and her excellent heart, was always an asset.

There are two notable reasons for believing that this woman possessed the rare ability to lead without offending or displaying herself. One reason is the apparent harmony between Priscilla and her husband. Obviously, because it is her name and not his which has been kept alive down through the years, she must have been the outstanding one of the two—at least where her ability was concerned. The church in Rome was named for Priscilla, not Aquila. Tertullias wrote of her, not her husband. The catacomb in Rome was named for her, not Aquila. Without a doubt, he was a deeply devout follower of Jesus Christ, working alongside his wife with Paul in the work of the Early Church, with perhaps equal devotion, but possibly with unequal ability. That there was harmony between them, so that Paul felt easy about leaving the new church in their hands, is a first class tribute to Priscilla's ability to handle human relationships!

She must have understood her quiet, reserved husband. Surely she accepted him as he was and didn't try to make a fire brand of him. Even her husband could follow her thinking and her leadership without feeling inferior to her. This is true greatness in a woman, wherever it is found.

Another evidence of her ability to lead without offending is apparent in her brief but vital encounter with the highly educated young Alexandrian preacher, Apollos. The facts are: Priscilla straightened him out on his doctrine and made him like it! She did *not* offend Apollos. He believed her. She had lifted his sights, shown him how to lay hold of the power he needed in his ministry, and he was grateful, not insulted that God had used a mere woman to do this for him.

It has been said that Paul was never overly fond of women in general. But he loved Priscilla, as he loved some others among his Christian sisters. Paul could love them because these women, like Priscilla, had put their entire personalities under the control of the One who came back to them all forever at Pentecost.

He has come back to us, too. There is no excuse whatever for a Christian woman in any century, including our own, to be difficult to get along with because of her good mind or her leadership ability.

Anyone can be invaded by Love.

25. PHEBE

A Plain Woman With a Responsible Heart

On a winter day in the year A.D. 58, a plain, dependable
looking woman named Phebe, left her home in Cenchreae,
port of Corinth, as a member of a caravan moving northward toward Achaia and Macedonia. Women traveled by
land when possible in those days, and Phebe most likely
made the first lap of her important mission by camel and
donkey. She carried a minimum of luggage—only one
small pack animal was needed to handle her possessions—but securely fastened beneath the folds of her plain
blue cotton dress, she carried the precious letter which
Paul had trusted her to deliver personally to the Christians
in Rome.

Paul had not yet gone to Rome, but he longed to go, and
planned to at the first possible moment; so the personality
and disposition and faith of the woman he chose to repre-
sent him had to be thoroughly responsible. The imperial
post of Rome was not available for private letters, and Paul
must have thought a long time before deciding to send
Phebe. Not that she might not have come to his mind first
of all, but she was a woman, and travel in those days was
dangerous and hard enough for men.

Phebe and Paul were friends—he could rely utterly on
this woman. She had given him chance after chance to
discover her generous, sensible heart. Toward the end of
the long letter she carried tucked inside her dress, Paul
wrote of her as "our sister." In all ways, Phebe had been
Paul's true sister in Christ Jesus. She not only carried a full
and responsible load of work in the church at Cenchreae in
Corinth, but her home was always open to anyone who
needed care and love. In the King James Bible, Phebe is
called "a succourer of many." The "many" had to include
derelicts and undesirables, because her home city was a
port in Corinth, and seaports in those days were steeped in
violence and wickedness. Escaped prisoners and drunken
sailors and the women who followed them were as wel-

come with Phebe as they would have been with the Lord she loved. They were also as welcome as some of the saints in the church there, and saints then, as now, could not have all been pleasant, lovable people.

Phebe had also cared for Paul. He was no longer young, and his general health, as well as his eyes, had failed. Paul's travel schedule alone must have tired him to illness at times. But as with Lydia and Priscilla, Phebe was always glad to welcome him, to minister to his needs.

Phebe was genuinely Christian. Paul could trust her not only to get his vital letter into the hands of the Roman Christians, but to guard the reputation of Jesus Christ among them. She was the natural, balanced kind of woman who didn't need to panic and wonder and struggle in prayer for the success of her mission. Phebe's trust was complete. She simply went when Paul asked her to go, trusting God to get her there.

He did. Most likely Phebe made the last lap of her journey by boat, across the narrow waters from Macedonia into the Roman Empire, but she got there, delivered the epistle to the Romans intact, and now it is ours, too.

*　　　*　　　*

Beyond the brief but loving reference to Phebe in the closing paragraphs of Paul's letter to the Roman Christians, there is no other mention of her in the New Testament. We do not know whether she stayed in Rome, or returned to her home city in Corinth. This is really not important. Wherever Phebe was, she continued to be Phebe, God's woman through and through.

Friendship was never a problem for her, because God controlled her entire personality. No one bothered to wonder if Phebe would be there on time or at all—she was God's woman and dependable twenty-four hours a day.

She may have been a woman of means, who could afford to pay her own way on this long journey from Corinth to Rome, or they may have had to take a collection at Corinth to send her. This is also unimportant. Aside from the fact that our debt to her is great (if she had failed we might not have the Book of Romans in our Bible!), the important thing about Phebe is Phebe herself.

Most women long for importance. All women want to be loved and needed for themselves. This is normal and natural. But I doubt that Phebe ever gave it a thought. She was too busy being concerned for everyone around her—great like Paul, or insignificant like a sailor's girl friend—to think much one way or another about whether or not she was needed.

In letter after letter I learn of women who are dissipating their energies and their time worrying about the fact that God may not be using them. Phebe lost no time or energy in this foolish fashion. She simply gave Him full control and went about her business, with little or no thought of herself except as she was helping or hindering the cause of Christ. I doubt that she thought much about that either. She had become a natural child of God, certain through every minute of her life of His constant care and concern for her, no longer needing to fret and stew about her own faith or the condition of her spiritual life. She was His, and she could always trust Him in every situation. Phebe had learned that true spirituality is not gauged by how much she strained toward God, by the high appearance of her own spiritual pursuits or the scope of her service. She had learned that true spirituality comes only when we have settled it once and for all that God is always mindful of us through every minute. Phebe had obviously learned that true faith is not measured by how much we concentrate on God, but by the extent of our knowledge that God is always concentrating on us.

Phebe rested in Jesus Christ, therefore Paul could rest in Phebe. More and more I am seeing that we become dependable and responsible according to how deeply we believe in the dependability and responsibleness of God!

If Phebe returned to Corinth, we can know she went right on being Phebe, God's woman. If she stayed in Rome, the same. God Himself was Phebe's home, and the ground on where she stood was holy ground. She did not demand to choose her scene of service, she served where she was, knowing He was there, too, needing her as she needed Him.

A true woman of God rests in the midst of any difficulty because she has discovered the magnificent quiet at the heart of this mutual need shared with the Lord God.

26. EUNICE AND LOIS

Two Women Who Loved One Boy

In about the year A.D. 48, when Paul was in Lystra on his first visit, Timothy, a boy of fifteen, was converted to faith in Jesus Christ. On his second visit to Lystra, Paul had just lost the help of Barnabas, who had been working and traveling with him. Instead of giving the faithful apostle a new brother, God gave him a son. To Paul, Timothy's conversion was no ordinary event. He loved this boy as though he had been his own son. Undoubtedly Paul stayed in the home where Timothy lived with his grandmother, Lois, and his mother, Eunice, and part of Paul's attachment for the boy had its roots in his admiration and respect for these two women.

They had lived together since the death of Timothy's Greek father, when Timothy was still a baby, and the three—mother, son and grandmother—were bound together in a close, love-filled family unit. From infancy, Timothy had been trained in the Scriptures, since his mother and grandmother were devout Jews. God was not new to the boy at his conversion, but God was now His Saviour, in Jesus Christ, and all the unusual spiritual traits which the lad possessed, were unified in one new nature in Christ.

"Fifteen is a marvelous age to have found Him," his wise old grandmother may have said. "Your mind is still young and pliable, your habits of worship can be easily strengthened—your faith can grow now for all the long years of your life, Timothy."

The boy had been reared in real harmony. Here was a mother and daughter who shared the strongest bond of love in their mutual love of the Lord God. They, too, through Paul, discovered the God of Israel in Jesus Christ, and the solemn, worshipful atmosphere of their devout home had added to it the bright new joy of the Messiah's coming. The three were closer together now than ever before, their home life happier. Timothy actually had two mothers, because his grandmother, Lois, had been a mother to him during the long hours in which Eunice had been forced to work in order to support them. They were his loved ones and he was theirs. People admired or envied this threesome where the usual human relationship problems seemed to have no place.

Theirs was the kind of home a boy never wants to leave. And yet, after prayer and a long talk with Paul, their beloved friend, the decision was made.

"I need him," Paul had said. "I cannot manage alone any longer. There is still much work to be done, and I need a boy like Timothy."

The tall, slightly built young man looked from his mother to his grandmother, respectfully waiting for one of them to speak first.

"If you say you need him," his mother Eunice said at last, "that is the same as God saying it, brother Paul."

Tears filled old Lois' eyes, but she added: "We know you don't make decisions like this without God's word for it, Paul. We will miss him—but the boy will go with you."

The morning Paul and Timothy sailed was exhilarating and happy, full of tears of joy and sadness. Timothy's eyes shone with excitement. He loved and admired Paul as though he were his own father. For one so young to be asked to work side by side with the great Apostle, was an honor. But he wore that honor, with dignity, and his youthful exuberance made Paul smile and it gave him courage.

Eunice and Lois checked his belongings once more. They had looked after him so long, neither of them dared to think of that part of the long months ahead. When such a thought stabbed their minds, they hid it quickly in their ample faith that God would take care of Timothy's needs now through other women whom he and Paul would meet along the way.

Lois brushed his blond hair down with her hand several times as the sea breeze kept mussing it up. Eunice asked several times if he was sure he had everything, and finally the boy walked energetically behind Paul onto the small wooden ship and was gone.

Tears flowed down the old withered cheeks and the young firm cheeks of his grandmother and mother, as they waved until the ship was out of sight. He had been the center and the joy of their human lives, but they were not filled with self-pity as they walked slowly back to the empty house, arm in arm. They, too, were God's women, and if Paul needed Timothy, that meant God needed him, too.

*   *   *

The simple story of these two utterly unselfish women is a good one on which to end this book. Nothing dramatic happened to them. They are not remembered for their much serving or teaching of the multitudes. Eunice and Lois are remembered for their unselfishness. When God asked for their beloved Timothy, they let him go, and they sent him away *free* in his young heart, loaded with no false guilt at leaving them alone.

Much has been written concerning their thorough early training of this lad. They had so steeped him in the Hebrew Scriptures, that he was at home at once in the kingdom work of the Messiah for whom they had waited so long. They had taught him values and a sense of genuine responsibility. For this alone, Eunice and Lois are revered and remembered. Their lives bore endless fruit, but it was borne through Timothy. They neither took nor wanted any credit for it. Both women lived gladly in the background. And I do not believe it was any great effort for either of them. They *were* unselfish women.

With all my heart, I admire and revere them for the way in which they reared Timothy during his formative years. But I am struck freshly with the fact that the most important thing they did for this boy was to condition him to love! Traveling and speaking in the cause of Christ is difficult enough in our century, with travel so simplified. When Timothy and Paul moved about from city to city, the sheer physical hardships involved would have broken both the body and the spirit of any man whose central motivation was *not* love. "The love of Christ constraineth us," Paul wrote.

And Timothy had been conditioned by Eunice and Lois to love itself. Now that Timothy had discovered love to be a Person, Jesus Christ, he could be quickly and easily at home with Him. A man who worked as Timothy worked had to be certain of the love of God. Paul had learned that nothing could separate us from the love of God in Christ Jesus. Timothy, because Eunice and Lois had made him a home with love, grasped this quickly.

It is exceedingly difficult for anyone to believe that God

loves him, if he has not been conditioned to love at home during his early life. Timothy had no trouble here.

But not for one minute is there any indication that they had spoiled him! They cared for him, they enjoyed him with their whole hearts, but they truly *loved* the boy. Real love never pampers. Real love gives the loved one guidance and training, but always leaves him free to learn for himself. When Timothy waved good-by to his mother and grandmother that day, he *owned* his own faith in Jesus Christ. He did not leave with their faith, or with Paul's. He left with his own. And because he did, he left understanding that responsibility and the need for maturity go hand in hand with faith. He left with understanding in his heart that all these things are integral parts of love, the kind of *giving love* which the Messiah poured down from His cross upon us all.

Lois and Eunice did more than merely instruct this boy in morality and decency. *They conditioned him to love*; to receive love and to give it away. True love such as the kind they showered upon Timothy, inevitably begins to influence the loved one, too. This is the way God changes us from glory to glory. He simply persists in loving us into total redemption! Timothy not only knew how to receive love, he knew how to give it to others.

He had grown up knowing the atmosphere of love.

Paul loved the boy enough to call him "my beloved son." Timothy knew how to return Paul's love, and did. Their friendship lasted to the end of Paul's long life. Timothy stayed with him for longer periods than any of his other helpers. He could send Timothy into touchy situations in the new churches, not only because he could trust Timothy's understanding of the doctrine of Christ, but because he could trust Timothy always to act in the realm of love.

Timothy was at home there, because of Lois and Eunice.

Twentieth century women can do no greater thing than to create the climate of love in their homes. Love which spoils and pampers, weakens and hampers. Real love strengthens and matures and leaves the loved one free to grow.

If Jesus Christ is in the center of your home, love is there. But we need to be convinced as Paul was convinced, that "neither death nor life, neither angels nor mighty ones, neither present nor future affairs, neither powers of the heights nor of the depths, neither anything else created shall be able to separate us from the love of God that is in Christ Jesus our Lord."

We must be convinced of this, but we must stay alert every minute to co-operate with Him in the freeing, giving realm of love.

CHRISTIAN HERALD ASSOCIATION AND ITS MINISTRIES

CHRISTIAN HERALD ASSOCIATION, founded in 1878, publishes The Christian Herald Magazine, one of the leading interdenominational religious monthlies in America. Through its wide circulation, it brings inspiring articles and the latest news of religious developments to many families. From the magazine's pages came the initiative for CHRISTIAN HERALD CHILDREN and THE BOWERY MISSION, two individually supported not-for-profit corporations.

CHRISTIAN HERALD CHILDREN, established in 1894, is the name for a unique and dynamic ministry to disadvantaged children, offering hope and opportunities which would not otherwise be available for reasons of poverty and neglect. The goal is to develop each child's potential and to demonstrate Christian compassion and understanding to children in need.

Mont Lawn is a permanent camp located in Bushkill, Pennsylvania. It is the focal point of a ministry which provides a healthful "vacation with a purpose" to children who without it would be confined to the streets of the city. Up to 1000 children between the age of 7 and 11 come to Mont Lawn each year.

Christian Herald Children maintains year-round contact with children by means of a *City Youth Ministry.* Central to its philosophy is the belief that only through sustained relationships and demonstrated concern can individual lives be truly enriched. Special emphasis is on individual guidance, spiritual and family counseling and tutoring. This follow-up ministry to inner-city children culminates for many in financial assistance toward higher education and career counseling.

THE BOWERY MISSION, located at 227 Bowery, New York City, has since 1879 been reaching out to the lost men on the Bowery, offering them what could be their last chance to rebuild their lives. Every man is fed, clothed and ministered to. Countless numbers have entered the 90-day residential rehabilitation program at the Bowery Mission. A concentrated ministry of counseling, medical care, nutrition therapy, Bible study and Gospel services awakens a man to spiritual renewal within himself.

These ministries are supported solely by the voluntary contributions of individuals and by legacies and bequests. Contributions are tax deductible. Checks should be made out either to CHRISTIAN HERALD CHILDREN or to THE BOWERY MISSION.

Administrative Office: 40 Overlook Drive, Chappaqua, New York 10514
Telephone: (914) 769-9000